Georgia's
Constitution
and Government

Georgia's Constitution and Government

NINTH EDITION

Richard N. Engstrom

Robert M. Howard

Arnold Fleischmann

The University of Georgia Press

ATHENS AND LONDON

© 2014 by the University of Georgia Press

Athens, Georgia 30602

www.ugapress.org

All rights reserved

Set in 8.5/12 Stone Serif ITC Pro by Kaelin Broaddus

Printed digitally

Most University of Georgia Press titles are
available from popular e-book vendors.

Library of Congress Control Number: 2014932116

British Library Cataloging-in-Publication Data available

CONTENTS

PREFACE

The Significance of State and Local Governments

Colleges and universities across the country offer numerous courses on American government and politics. Many cover only the national government despite the ways that state and local governments affect our daily lives. These activities range from providing basic local services such as schools, streets, water, law enforcement, and fire protection to allocating state funding for higher education, highways, parks, prisons, and health.

Many Americans have an image of an enormous national government and forget the scope of their other governments. Including money paid to other governments, the fifty states spent $2 trillion in fiscal year 2011, while the more than eighty-nine thousand local governments in the United States spent more than $1.6 trillion. That combined total of $3.67 trillion was roughly the same as the federal government's $3.6 trillion in spending. Moreover, while the federal government had 2.8 million civilian employees in 2011, state governments employed 3.8 million workers, and local governments such as cities, counties, and school districts employed another 10.8 million.[1] Keep in mind that these data cover an economic downturn in which state and local governments experienced major cutbacks in spending and employment.

Georgia's Constitution Requirement

A state law requires graduates of public colleges and universities in Georgia to demonstrate proficiency with both the U.S. and Georgia Constitutions. This monograph is intended to assist students in satisfying that requirement, either in courses or by examination.

Reading Tips for Students

The headings and subheadings in this monograph highlight important features of Georgia's constitution and government. To help students prepare for a test, we have put some important terms **in bold** and have reproduced a list of them following this preface. Court cases throughout have been placed *in italics*. Instructors vary as to which terms they consider more important; some also might add other terms to the list. Instructors also differ in what they want students to know about a term, including information beyond its definition.

Some material in tables is not in the list of key terms. For example, court cases are covered in the reading, with major federal cases also summarized in tables 8–12. Some of the terms are also included in almost every American government textbook's chapters on the U.S. Constitution, federalism, civil rights, and civil liberties.

KEY TERMS

Below are the key terms printed in bold in the text, listed in the order you will find them while reading. As indicated at the outset, the list does not include court cases. Individual instructors may emphasize some terms more than others, or they might want students to know more than definitions.

federalism
unitary system
confederation
enumerated powers
elastic clause
supremacy clause
implied powers
Tenth Amendment
reserved powers
Fourteenth Amendment
dual citizenship
selective incorporation
police power
initiative
earmarks
separation of powers
judicial review
line-item veto
county-unit system
term limits
multimember districts
single-member districts
president of the Senate
speaker of the House

resolution
general legislation
local legislation
plural executive
elected constitutional officers
constitutional boards and
    commissions
trial courts
appellate courts
advisory opinion
superior court
probate court
Georgia Court of Appeals
Georgia Supreme Court
district attorney
grand jury
indictment
trial jury
local constitutional officers
special district
home rule
general obligation debt
revenue bond
SPLOST

general election

primary election

runoff

referendum

recall election

redistricting

gerrymandering

equal protection

poll tax

white primary

literacy test

property qualification

grandfather clause

Civil Rights Act of 1964

Voting Rights Act

eminent domain

SLAPP

search and seizure

cruel and unusual punishment

Georgia's
Constitution
and Government

CHAPTER 1

The U.S. Constitution and Federalism

Constitutions are important because they establish the basic rules of the game for many political systems. They specify the authority of government, distribute power among institutions and participants in the political system, and establish fundamental procedures for conducting public business and protecting rights. Just as drawing up or changing the rules can affect the outcome of a game, individuals and groups battle over constitutions, which can help determine who wins or loses politically.

When the U.S. Constitution was ratified in 1789, **federalism** was one of its most important elements. Federalism is a type of political system that gives certain powers to the national government, others to the states, and some to both levels of government. In addition to the United States, countries such as Australia, Canada, Germany, and Switzerland have federal systems. These differ from **unitary systems** such as those of Great Britain or France, where all authority rests with the national government, which can distribute it to local or regional governments. Federalism also contrasts with **confederations**, where all power is in the hands of the individual states, and the national government has only as much power as the states give to it. The United States used such a system during 1781–1788 under the Articles of Confederation, as did the Confederate States of America. During the 1990s, confederations were tried following the break-up of the national governments in the Soviet Union and Yugoslavia.

The U.S. federal system is not static; in fact, it has changed significantly over the years. Four key factors have had a major influence on the way federalism in the United States has developed: national supremacy, the Tenth Amendment, the Fourteenth Amendment (all three found in the U.S. Constitution), and state constitutions (covered in part 2).

National Supremacy

The U.S. Constitution's stability is due in large part to its broad grants of power and its reinterpretation in response to changing conditions. Article 1, Section 8 grants Congress a series of **enumerated powers** such as taxing, spending, declaring war, and regulating interstate commerce. It also permits Congress to do whatever is "necessary and proper" to exercise those enumerated powers. This language is referred to as the **elastic clause** because of its flexible grant of authority. Article 6 reinforces the power of the national government by declaring that the Constitution and federal law are "the supreme law of the land." This **supremacy clause** thus identifies the U.S. Constitution as the ultimate authority whenever there is a need to resolve a dispute between the national government and the states.

In an 1819 case, *McCulloch v. Maryland*, the U.S. Supreme Court adopted a broad view of the national government's powers when it decided that the elastic clause allows Congress to exercise **implied powers** that are not mentioned explicitly in the U.S. Constitution but that can be inferred from the enumerated powers. The supremacy clause and implied powers have been cornerstones for the expansion of the national government's powers. Congress occasionally has turned programs over to states, as it did with changes in welfare laws during the 1990s, and has imposed new requirements and costs on them, as it did under the No Child Left Behind Act adopted in 2002 and the Patient Protection and Affordable Care Act adopted in 2010.

The Tenth Amendment

The constitutions, laws, and policies of the states cannot contradict the U.S. Constitution. Thus, federalism allows states many opportunities to develop in their own way, but it always holds out the possibility that the federal government may act to promote national uniformity. Much of the debate over ratification of the U.S. Constitution focused on claims that the national government would be too powerful. This concern was reflected in proposals to add twelve amendments in 1789. Ten of the proposed changes were ratified by the states in 1791 and are commonly referred to as the Bill of Rights. The **Tenth Amendment** reads:

> The powers not delegated to the United States by the Constitution, nor prohibited by it to the States, are reserved to the States respectively, or to the people.

The amendment thus grants states **reserved powers**, but it does not define them. As one might expect, this has produced conflicts between the national and state governments, many of which have ended up before the U.S. Supreme Court. For much of the period from the 1890s through the mid-1930s, the Court restricted efforts by Congress to enhance the power of the federal government. Since then, the power of the national government has grown, although some recent court cases have favored the states.

The Fourteenth Amendment

In 1868, the national government's power over the states was strengthened by the addition of the **Fourteenth Amendment** to the U.S. Constitution. One of three amendments designed to end slavery and grant rights to blacks after the Civil War, the Fourteenth states in part:

> No state shall make or enforce any law which shall abridge the privileges or immunities of citizens of the United States; nor shall any State deprive any person of life, liberty, or property without due process of law; nor deny to any person within its jurisdiction the equal protection of the laws.

This language is a fundamental statement of the principle of **dual citizenship**: Americans are citizens of both the nation and their state, and they are governed by the constitutions of both governments. The U.S. Constitution guarantees minimum rights to citizens that may not be violated by the states. The states, however, may grant their citizens broader rights than are guaranteed by the U.S. Constitution.

The Fourteenth Amendment has had an interesting and controversial history. The U.S. Supreme Court generally has defined the amendment's somewhat vague guarantees in terms of other provisions found in the U.S. Constitution. Since 1925, the Court has employed a process known as **selective incorporation,** which incorporates into the meaning of the Fourteenth Amendment the protections offered by the Bill of Rights. It does this by applying these guarantees to the states on a selective (case-by-case) basis. Congress, too, has used the Fourteenth Amendment in support of laws that restrict the power of state and local governments.

CHAPTER 2

State Constitutions

States adopt their constitutions within the context of national supremacy; enumerated, implied, and reserved powers; dual citizenship; and the provisions of the Tenth and Fourteenth Amendments. Many state constitutions are modeled after the U.S. Constitution. State constitutions generally do not include implied powers. States also possess **police power**, namely, the ability to promote public health, safety, morals, or general welfare. The police power is among the "reserved powers" in the Tenth Amendment to the U.S. Constitution. States often delegate police powers to local governments.

Basic Differences in State Constitutions

Most state constitutions are extremely long, in contrast to the 8,700 words in the original U.S. Constitution. Major reasons for such lengthy constitutions are numerous amendments, extended sections about local governments, and the absence of implied powers. Unlike the U.S. Constitution, which has been amended only twenty-seven times, state constitutions are amended frequently. This often is done to make policy changes that would seem easier to bring about by passing a law. For instance, Georgia voters had to approve an amendment in 1992 to remove language in the state constitution that prevented creation of the Georgia lottery. Putting policies in constitutions makes it harder for opponents to change them, however. Alabama's constitution is the longest among the states because it includes numerous local amendments that cover only one county.

The absence of implied powers means that state constitutions tend to be more detailed and restrictive in defining the powers

TABLE 1

State constitutions as of January 1, 2010

State	Estimated number of constitutions	Number of words	Amendments
Alabama	6	376,006	880
Alaska	1	13,479	29
Arizona	1	47,306	151
Arkansas	5	59,120	99
California	2	67,048	527
Colorado	1	66,140	158
Connecticut	4	16,401	30
Delaware[a]	4	25,445	142
Florida	6	56,705	121
Georgia	**10**	**41,684**	**73**
Hawaii	1	21,498	110
Idaho	1	24,626	125
Illinois	4	16,401	12
Indiana	2	11,476	47
Iowa	2	11,089	54
Kansas	1	14,097	96
Kentucky	4	27,234	42
Louisiana	11	69,876	176
Maine	1	16,313	172
Maryland	4	43,198	228
Massachusetts	1	45,283	120
Michigan	4	31,164	30
Minnesota	1	11,734	120
Mississippi	4	26,229	125
Missouri	4	69,394	115
Montana	2	12,790	31

of government. In addition, the U.S. Constitution says nothing about local governments, which state constitutions often cover at great length.

Table 1 indicates the number of constitutions each state has had, as well as the length of the state's current constitution and the number of its amendments. Georgia is noteworthy in two ways. First, it has had ten constitutions; only Louisiana has had more. Second, Georgia's current constitution took effect in 1983, making it very new. Only Rhode Island can be considered "younger," following a major revision of its 1842 constitution in 1986.

TABLE 1 (continued)

State	Estimated number of constitutions	Number of words	Amendments
Nebraska	2	34,934	230
Nevada	1	37,418	137
New Hampshire	2	13,060	145
New Jersey	3	26,360	46
New Mexico	1	33,198	165
New York	4	44,397	220
North Carolina	3	17,177	31
North Dakota	1	18,746	154
Ohio	2	53,239	172
Oklahoma	1	81,666	193
Oregon	1	49,016	253
Pennsylvania	5	26,078	30
Rhode Island	3	11,407	12
South Carolina	7	27,421	498
South Dakota	1	27,774	217
Tennessee	3	13,960	39
Texas	5	86,936	474
Utah	1	17,849	117
Vermont	3	8,565	54
Virginia	6	21,899	48
Washington	1	32,578	106
West Virginia	2	33,324	71
Wisconsin	1	15,102	145
Wyoming	1	26,349	100

ᵃAmendments are not subject to voter approval.

SOURCE: The Book of the States 2013, 12–13.

Amending State Constitutions

PROCEDURES IN THE STATES

The states use various methods to amend their constitutions (see table 2). Unlike amendments to the U.S. Constitution, every state but Delaware requires voters to approve constitutional amendments. To submit a proposed amendment to voters, eighteen states require a simple majority of their legislators to vote in favor of doing so. Most states are more restrictive. Georgia is among the twenty-one states requiring two-thirds of its legislature to vote in

TABLE 2

Procedures for amending state constitutions

Legislative vote to submit amendment[a]	Voter ratification required				No voter participation
	Two-thirds on amendment	Three-fifths on amendment	Majority on amendment	Majority in election	
Three-fourths (1)[b]			Conn.[c]		
Two-thirds (21)			17[d]	Hi., Tenn., Wyo.[e]	Del.[f]
Three-fifths (10)	N.H.	Fla.	7	Ill.	
Majority (18)			17	Minn.	

[a]Eighteen states also allow citizens to use the initiative process to place amendments on the ballot.
[b]Number of states in parentheses.
[c]Requires three-fourths approval in one legislative session, but only a majority in two consecutive sessions.
[d]Method used in Georgia.
[e]Hawaii allows a lower percentage for amendments approved in two legislative sessions. Tennessee requires a majority on first passage in the legislature, but two-thirds on second passage.
[f]Ratification requires two-thirds approval in two sessions of the legislature.

SOURCE: *The Book of the States: 2013*, pp. 14–15.

favor of submitting a proposed amendment to its constitution. Some states impose the obstacle of getting an amendment approved in two different legislative sessions before it can be submitted to voters. Four states, but not Georgia, limit the number of amendments submitted to the voters at one election.

Forty-two states require that a simple majority of voters must vote yes on an amendment for it to be ratified. The other states use several alternatives. Two states require more than a simple majority, two-thirds in New Hampshire, for example, and three-fifths in Florida. A few states, such as New Mexico, require a simple majority to ratify most amendments but larger majorities to ratify certain types of amendments. Five states require approval by a majority of those voting in an election, not just those voting on the amendment. Thus, if people vote on highly visible offices such as governor but skip an amendment on the ballot, not voting on the amendment is the same as voting "no." Similarly, in Nebraska, those casting a "yes" ballot must be a majority on the amendment *and* thirty-five percent of the total voting in the election.

During 2012, 135 constitutional amendments were proposed across thirty-five states. Eighteen of the proposals were put on the ballot through the citizen initiative process. Of the 135 proposals, 92 were adopted (68 percent). Thirty of the proposed amendments dealt with government finance, taxation, and debt. Another 20 dealt with their state's bill of rights.[1]

AMENDING THE GEORGIA CONSTITUTION

The Georgia legislature can ask the state's voters to create a convention to amend or replace the Constitution. The General Assembly also can propose amendments if they are approved by a two-thirds vote in each chamber of the legislature--a procedure like that at the national level. The governor has no formal role in this process but may be influential in recommending amendments and mobilizing public opinion before voters go to the polls. Georgia is not among the eighteen states whose constitutions allow amendments through the **initiative** process, in which citizens circulate petitions to place proposed amendments on the ballot for voters to ratify or reject in a statewide referendum.

The U.S. Constitution requires ratification of amendments by legislatures or conventions in three-fourths of the states. In contrast, the Georgia Constitution requires ratification by a majority of the voters casting ballots on the proposed amendment. Such proposals are voted upon in the next statewide general election after being submitted to the electorate by the General Assembly (November of even-numbered years).

CHAPTER 3

Constitutional Development in Georgia

Replacing any state's constitution is a rare event. Amending a constitution is much more common. Both types of change, however, have produced long and often complicated documents. Efforts to amend constitutions, like those to replace them, are often linked to politics. This is true of Georgia's ten constitutions, each of which reflects a political response to some conflict, problem, or crisis.

Politics and State Constitutions

Unlike the U.S. Constitution, most state constitutions include a wide range of very specific policies. Of course, legislatures normally enact policies by passing laws. Why clutter up state constitutions rather than limiting them to more fundamental issues? Three reasons stand out: attempts to gain political advantage, responses to state court decisions, and efforts to meet the requirements of the national government. Georgia's constitution includes numerous examples of all three.

POLITICAL ADVANTAGE

Many policies in state constitutions result from efforts by groups to gain a strategic advantage over their political opponents. If a group can get its position on an issue written into a state's constitution, changing that policy becomes much more difficult. This takes advantage of the rules of the game by forcing the opposition in the future to pass its own amendment rather than simply enacting a law. Amendments adding policies to Georgia's constitution have included earmarking, tax breaks, issues of morality, and limits on decision making.

Like many state constitutions, Georgia's includes **earmarks**, requirements that revenues from certain sources be spent for designated purposes. Needless to say, earmarks can benefit specific interests. The most significant are motor fuel taxes, which Article 3 requires to be spent "for all activities incident to providing and maintaining an adequate system of public roads and bridges" and for grants to counties. Moreover, this money goes for these purposes "regardless of whether the General Assembly enacts a general appropriations Act."[1] Thus, the Constitution provides those interested in highway construction with a guaranteed source of funds.

In other cases, the Constitution merely permits the earmarking of funds.[2] For instance, it allows the General Assembly to use taxes on alcoholic beverages for programs related to alcohol and drug abuse. The legislature can also create a variety of trust funds for programs ranging from the prevention of child abuse to the promotion of certain crops. The 1983 constitution, like all of its predecessors since 1868, prohibited lotteries. After being elected in 1990, Governor Zell Miller convinced the General Assembly to submit a proposed amendment to voters to create state-run lotteries whose proceeds would be spent on education. That amendment was ratified by a narrow majority in November 1992 following a vigorous campaign. The 1992 amendment requires that net proceeds (after expenses and prizes) go to "educational programs and purposes," with the governor's annual budget including recommendations for using those funds.[3] An amendment approved in November 1998 further restricted the use of lottery funds.

The second type of political advantage is special tax treatment for various groups and activities. An example is the taxation of timber, one of Georgia's major industries. An amendment approved by voters in 1990 requires that timber be taxed at fair market value only at the time of its harvest or sale.[4] Previously, it was taxed annually at market value. This change produced a major drop in property taxes for some counties and school districts. The Constitution also requires that certain agricultural land be assessed at 75 percent of its value[5] and exempts part of the value of a disabled veteran's home from property taxes.[6] Other sections of the Constitution authorize rather than require the General Assembly to establish certain types of tax preferences, as with a 1988 amendment that applies to property on a historic register and a 1992 amendment that permits special treatment for heavy motor vehicles owned by nonresidents.[7]

A third type of political advantage occurs when groups are able to get their positions on controversial social issues included in state constitutions. This happened with the U.S. Constitution when the Eighteenth Amendment was added in 1919 to ban the sale of alcohol. The Eighteenth Amendment was repealed, however, by the Twenty-first Amendment in 1933. Similar provisions exist in Georgia. The 1983 constitution retained the prohibition against whipping as a punishment for a crime out of fear that the General Assembly might pass bills permitting whipping in schools or prisons.[8] In 2004, Georgia voters were asked by the legislature to vote on an amendment that would define marriage as the "union of man and woman." Even though Georgia already had a law banning same-sex marriage, the legislature voted to submit an amendment on the matter, which passed in every Georgia county and carried by 76–24 percent statewide.

A fourth type of political advantage can be secured through procedures. Most importantly, constitutions can specify who gets to participate in key decisions and can restrict the discretion of government agencies. For example, Article 4 of Georgia's constitution creates six state boards and commissions, and Article 8 creates two more for education. The Constitution also establishes important political ties between the State Transportation Board and the General Assembly, thereby reducing the power of the executive branch over highways. The Constitution also includes residency requirements such as mandating one member from each congressional district on certain boards and commissions and stipulating that at least one member of the Board of Natural Resources be from one of six coastal counties.[9] The Constitution limits the discretion of government agencies through requirements like the one that gives veterans preference in state civil service employment.[10] A 2012 amendment allows the state to approve charter schools, thus enabling their proponents to bypass local boards of education that might oppose them.

STATE COURT DECISIONS

A second reason for including policies in a constitution is to respond to a state court decision. For example, the Georgia Supreme Court might hold that a state law or an action by a local government violates the Georgia Constitution. The most permanent method to reverse the Court's action is to amend the state constitution. Perhaps the most unusual example relates to nude dancing, which the Georgia Supreme Court ruled was expressive conduct protected by the Georgia and U.S. constitutions. Opponents of nude dancing clubs looked for a way to drive them out of business and got the legislature to propose an amendment that would permit local governments to prohibit alcohol sales at clubs with nude dancing. Alcohol sales are not constitutionally protected, so regulating them is a way to try to drive nude dancing clubs out of business. Voters ratified the amendment in 1994, and the Georgia Supreme Court ruled that such alcohol bans are allowed under the Georgia Constitution.[11]

Several decisions by the Georgia Supreme Court during the 1980s created confusion about the ability of citizens to sue the state or its local governments, and an amendment that attempted to clarify the matter was ratified in 1990.[12] Similarly, the 1983 constitution added language to clarify a confusing series of cases regarding planning and zoning.[13] A 2008 Georgia Supreme Court decision limiting the funding that could be used for urban redevelopment led to an amendment approved by a narrow majority of voters.[14]

NATIONAL GOVERNMENT REQUIREMENTS

A third way in which politics can affect state constitutions is through efforts to satisfy some requirement of the national government. For example, the Georgia Constitution was amended in 1988 and 1992 to create a trust fund to provide medical services for the poor through the federal Medicaid program. Without the trust fund, money unspent at the end of the budgetary year would have to go to the state's general fund and could be used for any purpose, as specified elsewhere in the Constitution.[15] With the trust fund, the unspent money can be carried over to the next year to pay for medical care. Another example can be found in

Article 3, which is written to satisfy federal court decisions about how legislative districts must be drawn.

A Brief Comparison of the U.S. and Georgia Constitutions

Constitutions are not static. Georgia has had ten constitutions, and the current one has been amended more than seventy times during its first thirty years. In addition, Georgia's constitutions have evolved because of the ways they have been interpreted by the courts.

SIMILARITIES

The most obvious similarity between the Georgia Constitution and the U.S. Constitution is that each includes a bill of rights. These guarantees were added as the first ten amendments to the U.S. Constitution, whereas a bill of rights is included prominently in the Georgia Constitution as the first article.

Both constitutions provide for a **separation of powers** with distinct legislative, executive, and judicial branches. The U.S. president and Georgia's governor have substantial power to appoint officials and to veto bills, although there are some important differences, as discussed below. Both the U.S. Congress and the Georgia General Assembly are bicameral, and each calls its two chambers the senate and house of representatives. Finally, both governments allow for **judicial review** (the power of courts to declare acts unconstitutional). Georgia courts are given this power in the state constitution,[16] while at the federal level it was stipulated in 1803 by the Supreme Court itself in the case of *Marbury v. Madison*.[17]

DIFFERENCES

Perhaps the most noticeable difference between the two constitutions is how much longer Georgia's is, mainly because it includes many detailed policies. These range from specific taxes to sections on retirement systems, local government services, the state lottery, and even nude dancing.

The two constitutions also have both procedural and structural differences. One procedural distinction deals with constitutional amendments. Georgia voters must approve all amendments to the state's constitution. There is no comparable role for citizens in amending the U.S. Constitution, where amendments require a two-thirds vote in each house of Congress and then must be ratified by three-fourths of the states, in either their legislatures or conventions. Another procedural difference is that the Georgia Constitution requires the state to have a balanced budget, whereas the U.S. Constitution imposes no such limitation on the national government. The Georgia Constitution also grants the governor a **line-item veto** (the ability to kill a specific item in a spending bill), but the U.S. Constitution grants the president no such power over legislation passed by Congress.[18]

The structural differences between the two governments' corresponding three branches are striking. Unlike the national government, whose judges are nominated by the president and subject to Senate confirmation, Georgia's voters elect almost all of their judges on a nonpartisan ballot. In addition, Georgia's attorney general issues advisory opinions, which generally have the force of law unless reversed by a court. No comparable process exists at the national level.

The legislative branches of the national and Georgia state governments also have some interesting differences. All legislators in Georgia (both representatives and senators) serve two-year terms and are elected from districts based on population. This contrasts with the national government, where representatives serve two-year terms and senators serve six-year terms. Moreover, while members of the U.S. House are elected from districts based on population, two senators are elected from each state--the same number for California and Wyoming—which builds in a bias in favor of less populous states.

The most glaring difference between the two executive branches is that Georgia's does not have a cabinet system. The president has the authority to appoint and fire heads of almost all major federal agencies. In contrast, Georgia's voters elect six department heads (e.g., insurance commissioner). This plural-executive structure can make life difficult for a governor whose political party and views may not be the same as those of the elected department heads. The Constitution also requires that several other department heads be chosen by boards or commissions rather than by the governor or the voters.

Perhaps the most striking structural difference between the Georgia Constitution and the U.S. Constitution concerns local governments. Georgia's constitution is quite specific about the organization of local governments, the services they can provide, the ways they can raise and spend money, and similar matters. It even limits the maximum number of counties to 159. The U.S. Constitution never mentions local government. Thus, under the federal system, local governments are "creatures of the state," which means that they derive their powers from their state constitution and laws.

Georgia's Previous Constitutions

In addition to substantive differences, Georgia's constitutions vary in the methods by which they were drafted and approved (see table 3). Seven were written by conventions composed of elected delegates. Two were prepared by bodies whose members were either appointed or included because they held specific offices. The 1861 constitution (the fourth) was the first to be ratified by voters. The constitution of 1976 came about after Governor George Busbee asked the Office of Legislative Counsel to prepare an article-by-article revision of the Constitution of 1945 for the General Assembly.

Even before American independence in 1776, Georgia was hard hit by the various import taxes that had led to colonial protests. Public opinion in Georgia favored independence, and citizens mobilized to break with England. The first self-government in Georgia was defined by the Rules and Regulations of 1776. This short and simple document was written hurriedly and adopted before the signing of the Declaration of Independence. All current laws were maintained except those in conflict with actions taken by the Continental Congress. It declared that governmental authority resided within the state, not with the British monarchy, and that power originated from the governed. While this document was not officially a state constitution, many have noted that it served as one. The Declaration of Independence

TABLE 3

Georgia's ten constitutions

Year implemented	Revision method[a]	Major characteristics
1777	Convention	Separation of powers, with most power in the hands of the unicameral legislature.
1789	Convention	Bicameral legislature, which chose the governor; no bill of rights.
1798	Convention	Popular election of governor; creation of Supreme Court; greater detail than predecessors.
1861	Convention	Long bill of rights; first constitution submitted to voters.
1865	Convention	Governor limited to two terms; slavery abolished; Ordinance of Secession repealed; war debt repudiated; some judges elected.
1868	Convention	Authorization of free schools; increased appointment power for governor; debtors' relief.
1877	Convention	More restrictions on legislative power; two-year terms for legislators and governor; no gubernatorial succession; most judicial appointments by legislature.
1945	Commission	Establishment of lieutenant governorship, new constitutional officers, new boards, state merit system; home rule granted to counties and cities.
1976	Office of Legislative Counsel[b]	Reorganization of much-amended 1945 constitution.
1983	Select committee[c]	Streamlining of previous document, with elimination of authorization for local amendments.

[a]Group responsible for proposing new document.

[b]State employees, attorneys.

[c]Almost exclusively leaders from the three branches of state government.

SOURCE: M. Hill, *The Georgia State Constitution*, pp. 3–20.

prompted Georgians to establish a more permanent government, and the state adopted the first of its ten constitutions in 1777.

THE CONSTITUTION OF 1777

Georgia's first constitution included now familiar ideas such as separation of powers among the legislative, executive, and judicial branches of government; proportional representation on the basis of population; and provisions for local self-government. This constitution, like the Rules and Regulations of 1776, expressed little protection of individual liberties. Despite this omission, Georgia's political culture at the time was more liberal than other states', and the Constitution was written to empower the common man (although only white males at least twenty-one years of age who had paid property taxes in the previous year were permitted to vote). The Anglican Church was disestablished, and language in the document was easily understood. Local control of the judiciary was ensured in that no courts were established above the county courts.

The transition from the Rules and Regulations of 1776 to a new constitution in 1777 was little noted by citizens. This document governed the state until the demise of the Articles of Confederation. Georgia ratified the U.S. Constitution in January 1788 (the fourth state to do so) and redrafted the state constitution to reflect this monumental change in national government.

THE CONSTITUTION OF 1789

The constitution of 1789 provided for a bicameral legislature. Although it made some accommodations for representation on the basis of population in the House of Representatives, all legislative districts were drawn within counties, which could have from two to five representatives and one senator. Slaves were counted as three-fifths of a person, in accord with the U.S. Constitution and to meet the demands of landowners seeking to enhance representation for areas with large plantations. The state capital was moved to Louisville from Augusta; provisions were included to mandate public education at the county level; and new counties were created to be represented in the legislature.[19] In addition, the constitution authorized the legislature to elect the governor and most other state elected officials except the legislature itself. Qualifications for voting included race, age, residence, and the payment of taxes in the previous year.

THE CONSTITUTION OF 1798

The short life of the constitution of 1789 can be attributed to a scandal over land speculation by legislators. The constitution of 1798 was written by a convention and retained much of the language of the previous document. However, it was much longer due to its increased detail about the powers of the legislature. As time passed, this constitution was amended to permit more democratic requirements for voting, establish executive offices to handle some of the duties of the legislature, outlaw foreign slave trade, and establish local governments. The constitution of 1798 proved more enduring than its predecessors and remained in effect until the formation of the Confederacy in 1861.

THE CONSTITUTION OF 1861

Secessionist fever at the start of the Confederacy could hardly allow the state constitution to go untouched. T. R. R. Cobb, the main author of the Confederate Constitution, was also the author of the Georgia Constitution under the Confederacy. This constitution reduced the size of the state legislature by permitting senators to represent more than one county, and it increased the governor's power significantly. Additionally, it institutionalized judicial review and established state judgeships as elective offices.

The constitution of 1861 was Georgia's first to be submitted to the voters for approval in a referendum. It was also the first Georgia constitution with an extensive list of personal liberties, including freedom of thought and opinion, speech, and the press. Citizens were warned, though, that they would be responsible for "abuses of the liberties" guaranteed to them. Naturally, the Georgia constitution under the Confederacy incorporated the ideals of states' rights.

THE CONSTITUTION OF 1865

The constitution of 1865 was drafted by reluctant Georgians to accommodate the demands of Congress for readmission to the

Union. Only men who expressed moderate political beliefs before and after the war were permitted to work on the document, which included the abolition of slavery, repudiation of Civil War debt, and repeal of secession.

The new constitution did not repeal the Ordinance of Secession, which the North preferred as a way to state Georgia's loyalty to the Union. Also absent was enfranchisement of the state's black population, although this was not as likely to stir animosity in the North since blacks could vote in only six northern states at the time. These omissions put pressure on Georgia to rewrite its constitution just three years later, again to meet the requirements for reentry into the Union. The constitution of 1865 was viewed largely as the work of northern carpetbaggers trying to make quick fortunes in the postwar South or, worse yet in the eyes of many, scalawags (southerners willing to cooperate with Yankees).

THE CONSTITUTION OF 1868

When a constitutional convention was called in 1867, most of Georgia's popular leaders boycotted it. The state capital, at that time in Milledgeville, refused to accommodate many of the delegates, some of whom were black. Therefore, the convention was held in Atlanta, and the new constitution, perhaps in retaliation for the inhospitable treatment by the city of Milledgeville, specified Atlanta as the capital. The constitution of 1868 met the requirements of Congress for readmission to the Union and eliminated all debts incurred prior to 1865. Public education was also provided for, to be funded by poll and liquor taxes, although some time would pass before this policy actually was implemented. Black citizens were ensured equal rights, at least on paper, and property rights for women were upheld. Moreover, some attempts were made to enhance the business climate in order to build a stronger tax base.

Due to the high representation of poor and black citizens at this convention, the constitution of 1868 was a liberal document for the times, particularly after blacks were seated in the General Assembly in 1870. Overall, the new constitution was widely unpopular due to its compliance with northern demands, which were symbolized by the presence of federal troops until 1876. It remained a symbol of southern defeat until replaced in 1877.

THE CONSTITUTION OF 1877

Georgia's post-Reconstruction constitution returned to more conservative ideals. It reduced the authority of state officials and shifted power to the counties, most of which were rural. Most noteworthy was its not-so-subtle disenfranchisement of blacks and poor whites through the mandate that only those who had paid all back taxes would be eligible to vote. As the constitution of 1877 was being drafted, factionalism within the ranks of the Democratic Party erupted. Many who were sympathetic to old southern culture were reluctant to compromise with those who called for economic development and progressive policies. An agreement was reached to comply with northern demands for Reconstruction, as well as demands from more industrialized northern states that the South continue to supply raw materials. This compromise stirred up a faction of the Democratic Party known as Bourbons, who were dedicated to pre-Civil War agrarian economic and social norms, white supremacy, and local and state self-determination. Republicans found that the compromise left them with little power, and it was quite some time before the Republican Party reasserted itself in the state.

The constitution of 1877 was not well suited to changing conditions. For example, it forbade public borrowing, thereby eliminating the possibility of large-scale improvements in transportation or education financed by the state. It eventually included 301 amendments, many of which were temporary or dealt with local rather than statewide issues. Others made Supreme Court justices elected officials, established juvenile courts and a court of appeals, empowered an elected public service commission to regulate utilities, and modified the boards overseeing education.

This constitution also codified the system of representation under which the six counties with the largest population were to be represented in the lower house of the legislature by three persons each, the next twenty-six most populous counties by two each, and the remaining counties by one each. This 3:2:1 ratio became the basis for the Democratic Party's use of the county-unit system to elect statewide candidates--a custom that became state law in 1917 with passage of the Neill Primary Act.

Under the **county-unit system**, candidates for statewide office were chosen in primaries based on county-unit votes, which were similar to the electoral votes used to elect the U.S. president. Each county had twice as many unit votes as it had seats in the Georgia House of Representatives under the 3:2:1 formula. Because the Georgia Republican Party was almost nonexistent during this period, the real winner of an office was generally the candidate who won the statewide Democratic primary election.

Beginning in 1920, the eight largest counties had six unit votes, the next thirty counties had four unit votes, and the remaining counties had two unit votes. Thus, Fulton County, which had more than 6,000 voters go the polls in 1940, had six unit votes; Quitman and Chattahoochee Counties, which each had fewer than 250 voters go to the polls that year, had two unit votes apiece. A county's unit votes were awarded on a winner-take-all basis, which meant that the candidate finishing first got all of the unit votes. Under this system, voters living in urban areas were marginalized because candidates for statewide office could concentrate on rural areas and win a primary without getting a majority of the popular vote.

The county-unit system was especially important in electing governors. In 1940, the 121 counties with two unit votes had 43.5 percent of Georgia's population, but 59 percent of the unit votes. In contrast, Georgia's eight most populous counties, with six unit votes each, had 30 percent of the state's population but a mere 12 percent of the unit votes. In 1946, Eugene Talmadge finished second in the primary for governor by about six thousand popular votes. He won the Democratic nomination, however, by besting his opponent 242 to 146 in unit votes.[20] The county-unit system remained intact until 1963, when the U.S. Supreme Court held that this underrepresentation of urban areas violated the equal protection clause of the Fourteenth Amendment.

THE CONSTITUTION OF 1945

The constitution of 1877 lasted until 1945, albeit in much-amended form. Dissatisfaction with the 1877 constitution, a careful study of the document in the 1930s, and prodding by Governor Ellis Arnall had led to the creation of a twenty-three-member commission to draft a new constitution. The use of a commission rather than an elected convention reflected the governor's wish to depoliticize the constitution and bring it up to date, as well as the General Assembly's previous failure to muster the two-thirds vote required to call a convention.[21]

The new constitution made few substantive changes. Its main effect was to condense its heavily amended predecessor. Perhaps the most notable changes were the creation of the office of lieutenant governor and new boards of corrections, state personnel, and veterans services. One contested issue was the ban against governors succeeding themselves, which the General Assembly retained in the draft submitted to the voters. The new constitution also authorized women to serve on juries and gave home rule to local governments, which increased their authority. The document also addressed the controversial issue of the poll tax.

With a turnout of less than 20 percent of those registered, voters approved the document by slightly more than a three-to-two margin following an active campaign on its behalf. Georgia thus became the first state to adopt a constitution proposed by a commission rather than by an elected convention. The limits of this constitution emerged quickly. Within three years, the new constitution had added its first amendments, and a total of 1,098 amendments would be proposed between 1946 and 1974. Voters ratified 826, of which 679 (82 percent) were local in nature rather than statewide.

THE CONSTITUTION OF 1976

An effort to revise the 1945 constitution occurred during the early 1960s, but a federal court ruling prevented voters from considering it during the 1964 general election. Another attempt died in 1970 when the House but not the Senate approved a document for submission to the electorate.

After assuming office in 1975, Governor George Busbee asked the Office of Legislative Counsel to draft a revision of the 1945 constitution in time for the 1976 election. The proposal included no real changes, but it did reorganize the constitution on an article-by-article basis so that it was easier to understand and interpret. After some revisions by the General Assembly, voters approved the document in November of that year. Because the 1976 constitution remained substantively the same as its precursor, the General Assembly almost immediately set out to consider a more thorough revision, creating the Select Committee on Constitutional Revision during its 1977 session.

Georgia's Current Constitution

ADOPTION

Drafting the constitution of 1983 was a long and contentious process. In fact, the process is a good example of how factionalism can play a role in state politics. Amendments to the previous constitutions had been proposed by the legislature and approved through popular vote, with those proposals affecting the entire state appearing on the statewide ballot and those affecting only one county or city appearing on the ballot only in that location.[22] Because the 1945 and 1976 constitutions so restricted local governments, cities and counties often were forced to amend the constitution in order to make changes in taxation or municipal codes. Between 1946 and 1980, Georgians were asked to vote on 1,452 proposed amendments (1,177 of them purely local) and ratified 1,105.

The huge number of amendments created an unwieldy document understood by only the most diligent of constitutional students. Voters became so annoyed with the large number of proposals that they began to vote them down. In 1978, the statewide ballot included over 120 proposed changes in the state's constitution, one-third of which failed to pass.[23]

In the late 1970s, many Georgians were pleased when Governor Busbee sought to rewrite the constitution again, although he may not have realized the political difficulty of such a task. A Select Committee on Constitutional Revision whose members included the governor, lieutenant governor, speaker of the House, attorney general, and eight other elected officials debated the proposed constitution for three years. The Select Committee began work in May 1977 and appointed committees with broader citizen membership to revise individual articles for consideration by the General Assembly and the electorate. In November 1978, two articles were submitted to voters, who rejected them.

Subsequent efforts by the Select Committee and the 1980 session of the legislature failed to produce a new constitution. During its 1981 session, though, the General Assembly created a Legislative Overview Committee on Constitutional Revision, with thirty-one members from each chamber, to work with the Select Committee. These efforts produced a document that was approved in a 1981 special session and modified at the 1982 regular session of the General Assembly before being submitted to the electorate.

Like constitutional revisions generally, this one was quite political. Lobbyists and others representing specific interests were quick to get involved in the process. The 1981 special session was also an expensive one, with one estimate that it cost $30,000 per day.[24] A confrontation occurred between Speaker of the House Tom Murphy and Governor Busbee over the powers to be granted to the legislature under the new constitution. This debate was fueled by the fact that governors had built up many informal powers under previous constitutions, including the naming of presiding officers of the House and Senate, as well as most legislative committee and subcommittee chairs. This practice ended with the 1966 election, when the legislature chose Lester Maddox as governor because no candidate got a majority of the popular vote. The General Assembly also organized itself without input from the governor and gained more power in subsequent years. Thus, by the early 1980s, legislators wanted to guard their political gains, but Governor Busbee favored the delegation of some powers to bureaucratic offices and state boards. The governor and the General Assembly also disagreed over taxes and gubernatorial term limits. At one point, Busbee asked legislators to forget the proposal and spend the remaining days of the session on other topics.[25] Agreement was eventually reached, and voters approved the new constitution in November of 1982 by a nearly three-to-one margin. It took effect in July 1983.

MAJOR PROVISIONS OF THE 1983 CONSTITUTION

The 1983 constitution includes eleven articles, many of them detailed and complicated. Still, the document is much shorter than its predecessor and is written in simpler and gender-neutral language. Although it can be argued that the new constitution is one of evolution rather than revolution, it includes many noteworthy changes:[26]

- eliminating the requirement that local governments place changes in taxation, municipal codes, and employee compensation on the state ballot
- establishing a unified court system, consolidating the duties of justices of the peace and small claims courts into magistrate courts, and strengthening the state Supreme Court
- requiring nonpartisan election of state court judges
- enhancing the power of the General Assembly to enact laws and authorize the appropriation of taxes
- giving the Board of Pardons and Paroles power to stay death sentences
- including an equal protection clause ("No person shall be denied the equal protection of the laws"), which is like the guarantee in the Fourteenth Amendment to the U.S. Constitution
- reducing the total amount of debt that the state may assume
- providing more open-to-the-public committee and legislative meetings
- incorporating more formal separation of powers between the legislative and executive branches

The new constitution did not repeal the long list of local amendments to the old constitution. It simply allowed them to continue in force if approved by the General Assembly or the affected local government and froze them by prohibiting the addition of new local amendments.

CONSTITUTIONAL AMENDMENTS

As already noted, the General Assembly can submit a proposed amendment to voters if it wins a two-thirds majority vote in the House and the Senate, with the governor having no formal role

TABLE 4

Proposed amendments to the Georgia Constitution

Year	Number of amendments submitted to voters	Number ratified
1984	11	10
1986	9	8
1988	15	6
1990	9	8
1992	8	7
1994	6	5
1996	5	4
1998	5	3
2000	7	6
2002	6	4
2004	2	2
2006	3	3
2008	3	2
2010	5	3
2012	2	2
TOTAL	96	73

SOURCES: For 1984–1992, Hill, *The Georgia State Constitution*, pp. 20–23; for 1994, *Georgia Laws 1995 Session*, vol. 3, pp. cccxvii–cccxix; for 1996–2010, Georgia Secretary of State Elections Division, "Georgia Election Results," http://sos.georgia.gov/elections/election_results/default.htm.

in the process. The Georgia Constitution further requires ratification by a majority of the voters casting ballots on the proposed amendment. Such proposals are voted upon during the next statewide general election in November of even-numbered years (see table 4).

Despite the relatively young age of the Georgia Constitution, efforts to amend it have become somewhat common, although the number of proposals has not reached the dizzying heights of the previous constitution. Of ninety-six proposed amendments on the ballot between 1984 and 2012, voters approved seventy-three (76 percent). At least two proposals were on the ballot each year, with a high of fifteen in 1988.

The 2002 election included six proposed amendments. By relatively thin margins, voters rejected two proposals dealing with taxation of low-income residential developments and commercial docksides used in the landing and processing of seafood.

Voters did approve two amendments to provide tax incentives for the redevelopment and clean-up of deteriorated or contaminated properties, another amendment to establish a program of dog and cat sterilization funded by special license plates, and a measure to prohibit individuals from holding state office if they have defaulted on their federal, state, or local taxes.

The November 2004 ballot included only two proposed amendments. One was a rather obscure question regarding the jurisdiction of the state Supreme Court. The other, however, was a contentious measure banning same-sex marriage. It passed state-wide with 76 percent in favor, and received a majority in all 159 Georgia counties, with the closest margin being 52–48 percent in Athens-Clarke County.

The three amendments proposed in 2006 could be considered symbolic, in that they were of limited substantive effect. One, written in response to a U.S. Supreme Court decision, restricted the ability of government to seize private property. The other two dealt with hunting and fishing rights and special vehicle license plates. The first two passed with over 80 percent in favor, while the license plate measure breezed through with 67 percent in favor.

All three amendments on the 2008 ballot were related to growth and development. The first asked voters to approve a tax break for large tracts of timber owned by companies. Individually owned timber already had a similar tax break, and the amendment was ratified by more than two-thirds of those voting on it. The second proposal sought to allow school districts to freeze their property tax revenue in areas being developed until the infrastructure improvements were paid off. After that, the districts would collect taxes based on the value of the land after the improvements. Cities and counties could already do this, but the Georgia Supreme Court ruled in 2008 that school districts could not.[27] This amendment passed with a narrow majority. The final amendment was designed to allow developers to levy fees to pass along the cost of improvements in subdivisions to new home-buyers. Voters rejected this proposal, with a majority of just 51.6 percent.

The legislature asked voters to consider five amendments in

November 2010. Voters rejected a proposal for a ten-dollar vehicle tag fee to fund trauma care, with 52.6 percent opposed. This was despite supporters' spending more than $3.7 million on the campaign.[28] The other failed proposal (50.1 percent opposed) related to state contracts for long-term transportation projects. The other three proposals passed with more than 60 percent of the vote. They dealt with court enforcement of contracts, energy conservation, and zoning.

The November 2012 ballot included only two proposed amendments. One covered the contentious issue of creating local charter schools with limited connection to local public school systems. It allowed charter school applicants to bypass local school boards and seek state approval for new charter schools. The amendment passed with 58.6 percent in favor statewide.

From the voter's perspective, few of the amendments proposed over the past decade seem like burning issues at the core of what state government does or how it operates. Nevertheless, Georgia is like most states in that its constitution includes narrow topics that many people would expect could be addressed simply by adopting, changing, or repealing laws and regulations.

CHAPTER 4

Georgia's Governmental Institutions

Like most states, Georgia's constitution mirrors the separation of powers adopted by the framers of the U.S. Constitution. Perhaps the most important aspect of the Georgia Constitution is what Melvin Hill calls its status as "a power-limiting document rather than a power-granting document."[1] Thus, many provisions specify things that the state of Georgia and its local governments *cannot* do.

The Georgia Constitution spells out the organization and authority of the legislative branch in Article 3 and of the judicial branch in Article 6. Beyond that, the organization of government looks a bit different than at the national level. Executive responsibilities are spread among provisions in Article 4, which covers six boards and commissions, and Article 5, which encompasses the governor, lieutenant governor, and the six elected department heads. Other provisions affecting administration and local government are found in Article 8, which covers Georgia's system of education. Local government is covered in Article 9, which comprises almost 20 percent of the Constitution.

The Georgia General Assembly

COMPARISONS TO CONGRESS AND OTHER STATE LEGISLATURES[2]

On the surface, there are few differences between the U.S. Congress and Georgia's legislature, which is officially named the Georgia General Assembly. Both are bicameral. The presiding officer of the House of Representatives is called the speaker and is chosen by the members, and the leader of the Senate (vice president of the United States and the lieutenant governor of Georgia) is elected independently of its members.

Unlike Congress, where the entire House and only one-third of the Senate are elected every two years, all 236 members of the General Assembly are up for election every two years. The General Assembly also meets for a very limited time each year, and its members do not enjoy the high salary and sizeable staffs of members of Congress and some state legislatures. Because of the comparatively low pay and part-time nature of the job, the Georgia General Assembly is among the legislative bodies labeled "amateur" rather than "professionalized" by political scientists. This is in contrast to states like California and New York, where the legislature meets year-round and being a member is a well-paid, full-time job.

The Georgia General Assembly has much in common with other state legislatures. Its members are charged with representing the people of their districts, reapportioning legislative seats following the census conducted every ten years, enacting laws, adopting taxing and spending measures, overseeing enforcement of current laws, and assisting constituents. Except for Nebraska, every state legislature is bicameral, elects its members on a partisan basis, and has an upper chamber called the senate. Forty-one states call their lower chamber the house of representatives. Georgia is among the forty-two states that annually convene regular legislative sessions. The fact that only eight state legislatures still meet biennially reflects the view that meeting once every two years may be too infrequent to keep up with problems in the modern world.

Differences do exist among legislatures, however. The number of members varies from a low of 49 in Nebraska's unicameral legislature to a high of 424 in the small state of New Hampshire. Georgia, with its 236 members, has the third-largest legislature. The average senate (including Nebraska's unicameral legislature) has 39 members, as compared to Georgia's 56. For the forty-nine bicameral legislatures, the average house of representatives has 110 members, much smaller than the 180 found in the Georgia House.[3]

Qualifications such as minimum age, length of residence, terms of office, and term limits vary. Georgia is one of eleven states using only two-year terms. Members of Nebraska's unicameral legislature serve terms of four years; four states have four-year terms for both chambers; the remaining thirty-four states elect their upper chamber to four-year terms and their lower chamber to two-year terms. Unlike fifteen other states, neither Georgia's constitution nor its laws impose legislative **term limits**, which set a maximum number of terms (or consecutive terms) that an elected official can hold an office. Those who back term limits see them as a way to use turnover in membership to promote competition in elections and to make it harder for a legislator to become a career politician. In states with such restrictions, members who reach their limit in one chamber often run for the other (representatives run for the senate and vice versa) or seek another office.[4]

Regular legislative sessions range from off-year limits of thirty calendar days in New Mexico and Virginia and twenty legislative days in Wyoming to unlimited duration for annual sessions in thirteen states. Georgia is somewhere in the middle, with an annual session of forty legislative days. Leadership, procedures, and compensation also vary widely among the states.

REPRESENTATION

Georgia's earliest legislatures were based on county representation, initially with at least one representative for each county. This meant that the size of the General Assembly fluctuated over the years as new counties were created or counties were allotted additional seats. During the 1960s, for example, the House had over two hundred members at one point. Senate districts had three counties, and each seat rotated among its three counties at the end of each term. With each senator serving only one term and then giving way to someone from a neighboring county, power in the legislative branch was concentrated in the House, where members could serve an unlimited number of terms.[5]

The constitution of 1983 restricted the Senate to not more than 56 members, while the House must have at least 180 members (size can be changed by law within these limits). Reapportionment occurs every ten years, following the U.S. census. The General Assembly has substantial flexibility in drawing legislative districts. This authority became more limited beginning in the 1960s, though, when federal courts ruled that all representation within state legislatures must be based on population rather than county, and Congress adopted the Voting Rights Act, which was passed in 1965 to ensure minority representation as the South desegregated.[6] The practice of rotating Senate seats among counties in a district ended, which allowed senators to run as incumbents and increased the power of the Senate.

After the 1990 census, the legislature abandoned **multimember House districts**, which elected several representatives within the same district, requiring instead that candidates run for a designated seat. For example, people running for District 72, Post 1 did not compete with candidates for District 72, Post 2, although the electorate consisted of the same voters. With two seats, District 72 would have two seats and twice the population of a **single-member district**, where voters would elect only one House member. During its 2001 session on redistricting, the General Assembly created more than twenty large, multimember House districts where voters would elect two, three, or four representatives. Subsequent litigation, however, modified the boundaries for both Senate and House seats, and multimember House districts were eliminated.[7]

The most recent census was taken in the spring of 2010. The November 2010 election put the Republican majority in the Georgia House and Senate in a position to redraw districts for the U.S. House and their own seats in the General Assembly for the 2012 elections, which can affect the fortunes of incumbents, political parties, and a wide range of interests for the rest of the decade. Georgia's population growth between 2000 and 2010 earned the state one more seat in the U.S. House. With a total population of over 9.7 million in 2010, each of the 14 U.S. districts would have approximately 695,000 people. In the General Assembly, the 56 Senate districts would average almost 174,000 people, while the 180 House districts would each have around 54,000 residents.

QUALIFICATIONS OF MEMBERS

Article 3, section 2 of the Georgia Constitution requires that those seeking office in the General Assembly be registered voters, U.S. citizens, and Georgia citizens for at least two years. It also requires that representatives live within their districts for at least one year.

Those elected to the Senate must be at least twenty-five years old, while members of the House must be at least twenty-one. Persons may not simultaneously run for more than one office or in the primaries of two political parties. Also ineligible to serve are people on active military duty, those who hold other elected or civil offices within the state (unless they resign), and convicted felons.

LEGISLATIVE SESSIONS

The Georgia General Assembly meets annually in a regular session that begins on the second Monday of January and lasts up to forty legislative days. These are not calendar days, but days that the General Assembly is in session (not in recess or adjourned). The General Assembly may be called into special session by the governor, who sets the agenda, or by agreement of three-fifths of the membership of each chamber. Special sessions may be called to deal with unexpected crises such as natural disasters, budgetary shortfalls, or other state emergencies. Special sessions may not last longer than forty days and generally cannot be used for matters unrelated to the official agenda.[8]

LEGISLATIVE LEADERSHIP[9]

When members of the General Assembly arrive in Atlanta for the beginning of a new legislative session, their first priorities include selecting leaders and organizing committees. The Georgia Constitution provides for the selection of presiding officers in each chamber. In the Senate, the lieutenant governor serves as **president of the Senate**, just as the vice president of the United States is formally the presiding officer of the U.S. Senate. Thus, the presiding officer of the Senate is chosen by Georgia's voters in a statewide election, although the winner is chosen independently from the governor. It is worth noting that twenty-three other states (including Nebraska's unicameral legislature) also make the popularly elected lieutenant governor presiding officer of the senate. In the remaining twenty-six states, the senate chooses its own presiding officer. The Georgia Senate also elects one of its members as president pro tempore should the need arise to replace the presiding officer.

The members of the Georgia House elect the **speaker of the**

House from among their members, as do the lower houses in the other forty-eight bicameral legislatures and the U.S. House of Representatives. In Georgia, House members also elect a speaker pro tempore, as do those in twenty-five other states; the remaining twenty-three legislatures either have no such position or require their speaker to appoint someone. In the speaker's absence, the speaker pro tempore presides.

The Constitution says little about the powers of legislative leaders, which are detailed in the rules of the House and Senate. For example, beginning in 2003, the Georgia Senate stripped the lieutenant governor of significant power over the make-up and leadership of committees.[10]

TYPES OF LEGISLATION

Article 3 of the Georgia Constitution includes several sections detailing the General Assembly's procedures and powers for enacting laws, conducting impeachments, and spending public money. Bills before the General Assembly can be classified as resolutions, general legislation, and local legislation. All currently enforceable statutes are published in the *Official Code of Georgia Annotated*, which is updated periodically to include both new laws and legal opinions on implementation of current law.

Much of what passes through the General Assembly is not intended to be implemented as law. Some items brought up for consideration are intended as statements of legislative opinion and may be enforceable only on the membership of the legislature itself. For example, the legislature may wish to recognize individuals or a sports team, in which case the General Assembly might pass a **resolution** describing the honoree's achievements. Resolutions also might be used to create special committees, to determine compensation for citizens who have been injured or suffered damages by state actions, or to set requirements for legislative staff. The resolution would therefore have little impact on other citizens of the state. It would, however, express the approval of the state government.

Resolutions might be passed to require the General Assembly itself to behave in a specific manner, as with rules of conduct, scheduling, or agreements on budgetary matters. In some cases, resolutions are passed by one chamber to establish rules only for that chamber's own membership, but joint resolutions require passage through both chambers. Resolutions generally do not require the signature of the governor because they do not require implementation outside the legislature itself. However, joint resolutions that are enforceable as law do require the governor's signature and may be vetoed.

General legislation has application statewide. Laws regarding election procedures or speed limits on state highways are examples. Local governments may not pass ordinances that contradict general law. Most general legislation intended to change existing law will specify exactly which statutes will be changed, but any new legislation supersedes past legislation.

Laws passed by the Georgia General Assembly that apply only to specific cities, counties, or special districts are referred to as **local legislation**. The General Assembly retains the power to govern localities through the passage of local legislation.[11] Local legislation may not contradict general legislation and may not be used to change the tenure of particular local officials. It can, however, be used to create or change political boundaries. The passage of local legislation differs in some ways from the passage of general law. Local bills must be preceded by a period of advertisement in which citizens of the jurisdiction concerned are notified of the potential law. This most often occurs in local newspapers.

CONSIDERATION OF BILLS

Only members of the General Assembly may introduce legislation, although by custom governors have had members introduce bills on their behalf. Bills may be sponsored by multiple legislators and may be introduced in either chamber of the General Assembly or at the same time in both chambers. One exception is legislation dealing with public revenues or the appropriation of public money, which the Constitution requires to begin in the House of Representatives.[12]

Bills must adhere to a specific format dictated by the Constitution and the rules of each chamber. The title of the bill must relate directly to its content, and bills are constitutionally restricted to no more than one purpose. The Constitution forbids the introduction of bills that deal with specific individuals or might limit the constitutional authority of the General Assembly. Population bills (those that apply to jurisdictions of a certain population) are also forbidden, as are bills that would have the effect of limiting business competition or creating monopolies within the state.

The Constitution mandates that all general legislation be read three times from the floor on three separate days. Because the title is required to be a summary of intent, reading the title only is substituted for the first reading of the entire bill. A second reading of the bill, which occurs on the second day after introduction, will also be of the title only. Local legislation may be voted on after only one reading. The media may follow the passage of a bill, and the Constitution requires that floor action and committee meetings must be "open to the public," but this guarantee is not absolute.[13]

Bills are passed by a simple majority of the entire membership of each chamber, although there are several exceptions to this rule. Tax legislation, proposed amendments to the Constitution, veto overrides, punitive action taken against a member of the General Assembly, or motions to change the order of business require two-thirds majorities. Bills that have been rejected once in a legislative session also require a two-thirds majority to be reconsidered. Procedural changes may only require a majority of those members present. Once a bill has achieved a majority vote in one chamber, it must be passed in identical form by a majority vote in the other chamber in order to continue on the path to becoming a law.

THE STATE BUDGET

The budget is a special type of lawmaking. The Georgia Constitution directs the governor to prepare the state's annual budget and submit it to the General Assembly during the first five days of the regular legislative session.[14] This leaves the governor with substantial authority in the early stages of drafting the budget. This is countered, however, by the legislature's virtually unlimited power to change the budget submitted by the governor. Georgia's governor can exercise a line-item veto in an attempt to remove specific spending without vetoing the entire budget. Like a regular veto, the line-item veto can be overridden by a two-thirds vote of the membership in each chamber of the General Assembly.[15]

The Constitution also requires that the state adopt a balanced budget, something the federal government is not obligated to do. However, a balanced budget does not mean that the state does not have debt. Like most state and local governments, Georgia sells bonds to investors to pay for large projects. The state then pays off the bonds over time, much like a family pays off a mortgage. The state then includes its debt payments as part of the annual balanced budget that it must adopt.

The Executive Branch

One of Georgia's most striking differences with the U.S. government is the state's number of elected officials in the executive branch. The most visible executive offices in Georgia are the governor and the lieutenant governor. While they may be compared to the U.S. president and vice president, they are not elected together as a team and may represent different political parties and viewpoints.

Like the majority of states, Georgia has a **plural executive**, meaning that voters elect various department heads, whereas presidents choose members of their cabinet (see table 5).[16] In fact, voters around the country choose over five hundred officials in statewide elections (a number virtually unchanged since the mid-1950s). Some of these officials are required by state constitutions to be elected; others are provided for by law. Their tasks vary significantly. Financial monitoring, for instance, is assigned to elected auditors, comptrollers, and treasurers in some states but is the responsibility of appointed officials in others. A few states elect boards to govern public education, while Colorado, Michigan, and Nebraska voters elect boards to run their state universities.[17] At the other extreme, the governor is the only elected executive in Maine, New Hampshire, and Tennessee. Voters in Alaska, Hawaii, and New Jersey also elect a lieutenant governor.

<u>TABLE 5</u>

Executive branch officials elected by the public

Office	Number of states electing	Georgia
Governor	50	elected statewide
Lieutenant governor	43[a]	elected statewide
Attorney general	43	elected statewide
Secretary of state	35	elected statewide
Education superintendent	14	elected statewide
Agriculture commissioner	13	elected statewide
Insurance commissioner	12	elected statewide
Labor commissioner	5	elected statewide
Utilities regulation	6	5 commissioners elected statewide
Treasurer	36[b]	appointed by a board
Auditor	23[b]	chosen by legislature

[a]Lieutenant governors are included despite their role as presiding officers in legislatures because of their right to succeed governors and their executive responsibilities in some states. The total does not include Tennessee or West Virginia, where the state senate chooses a presiding officer who is considered lieutenant governor.

[b]Some responsibilities of auditors and treasurers are assigned to an elected comptroller in ten states, and to the chief financial officer elected in Florida.

SOURCE: *The Book of the States 2013*, 171–76, 190–92.

THE GOVERNOR

Governors are generally the most powerful political figures in their states. Their political clout is based on the formal authority granted in the state's constitution, but it is balanced against the authority of other institutions, including the legislature and the courts. Beyond their constitutional powers, governors also develop political power based on laws, the media, public opinion, ties to political parties and interest groups, and their personal characteristics.

Professor Thad Beyle originally developed a scoring system for comparing the formal power of the nation's governors, including their tenure potential, appointment powers, budgetary control, veto power, and the number of separately elected executive officials.[18] The tenure potential (number of consecutive terms permitted for a governor) has been a contentious issue in Georgia's political history. The 1877 constitution limited the governor to two consecutive, two-year terms. A 1941 constitutional amendment provided for a four-year term but prohibited governors from succeeding themselves in office. That was changed in 1976 to permit successive terms, but the lifetime limit for any governor was also two terms. The constitution of 1983 permits two consecutive, four-year terms with no lifetime restriction on the time of a governor's service. That earned Georgia's governor a score of 4 on Beyle's 5-point scale for tenure potential. In comparison, eleven states earned scores of 5, allowing their governors to serve an unlimited number of four-year terms. At the opposite pole is Virginia, which does not allow governors to succeed themselves.[19] The Georgia Constitution does not limit the number of consecutive terms that other statewide elected officials can serve, and some have held their posts for decades.

In terms of appointment power, Georgia's governor earned a very low score of 1.5 because of limited power in six key areas: health, education, transportation, corrections, public utilities regulation, and welfare. The average among the fifty states is 2.85 on a 1–5 scale. In Georgia, gubernatorial control over boards and commissions is weakened because terms are long and staggered, which means that some time can pass before a governor's appointees are in control. In the case of one board (transportation), the governor does not even appoint the members--the General Assembly chooses them. Again using a 5-point scale to measure the extent to which executive branch officials are separately elected, Georgia's governor received the lowest possible score of 1 because of the plural executive. This compares to the four states getting a score of 5 because of their cabinet-style organization.

Perhaps the Georgia governor's most important appointment power is the constitutional authority to fill vacancies in the executive and judicial branches without Senate confirmation.[20] In the case of elected positions, the governor picks someone who finishes an unexpired term, thus becoming the incumbent in the next campaign. By law, the governor also can fill vacancies at the local level when an official has been removed temporarily following an indictment.[21]

The 1–5 scale of budgetary power assigns a value of 1 to a governor who prepares the budget with other officials and faces unlimited legislative ability to amend it, while a 5 is assigned to the governor who prepares a budget that the legislature is prohibited from increasing. Georgia rated a 3 on budgetary powers: the governor has full responsibility for preparing the budget, but the legislature has unlimited ability to change it.

Using a similar 1–5 scale to rate veto power, Georgia's governorship scored a 2.5, meaning that the governor has line-item veto only for appropriations, but with a requirement for a large majority of the legislature to override (two-thirds of the total membership of each chamber). Twenty-five states make it easier to override a gubernatorial veto: seven require only a majority of legislators elected, six mandate three-fifths of those elected, and twelve specify three-fifths or two-thirds of those present for the override vote.[22]

The governor's veto power is included in the legislative, not the executive, article of the Georgia Constitution.[23] The governor has authority to act on legislation passed by the General Assembly that would have the effect of law, except for changes in the Constitution. If the governor signs a bill, it becomes law on a specified date, usually with the start of the fiscal year on July 1. The governor has six days to act on a bill while the General Assembly is in session. If the General Assembly has adjourned for the session or for more than forty days (in a recess, for instance), the governor has forty days after adjournment to act. When vetoing a bill, the governor is required to return it to the chamber where it originated within three days during the session or within sixty days after adjournment. Once the General Assembly has received a veto message, the originating chamber may consider the vetoed bill immediately. Those bills vetoed during adjournment can be overridden during the next legislative session, as long as an election has not intervened.

A bill also becomes law if the governor does nothing (neither signs nor vetoes it). If the governor fails to act on a bill, it will become law following a six-day waiting period for bills passed during the first thirty-four days of the legislative session, or following a forty-day waiting period for bills passed during the final six days of the session. Thus, bills may sit on the governor's desk after adjournment of the legislature and become law even if the governor does not sign them.

Georgia is among the forty-four states that provide for two types of vetoes, full and line-item. A full veto is a rejection of an entire bill. Line-item vetoes are rejections of specific passages in bills. In Georgia, the line-item veto applies only to appropriations bills; it allows the governor to kill specific spending for projects or programs without having to veto an entire state budget. Reconsideration of bills in which specific funding has been line-item vetoed is not necessary, and the governor's actions officially reduce the appropriation if not overridden. A successful override allows a bill to become law in spite of the governor's veto. If an override fails in either chamber of the Georgia General Assembly, the bill is dead.

THE PLURAL EXECUTIVE

The Georgia Constitution requires voters to elect six department heads in addition to the governor and lieutenant governor. Together, these eight officials are referred to as the state's **elected constitutional officers**.[24] Like a majority of states, Georgia elects an attorney general and secretary of state. Georgia is among the few states, however, where voters pick a state school superintendent and heads of the departments of agriculture, insurance, and labor.[25]

Georgia's elected department heads must have reached the age of twenty-five and must have been a U.S. citizen for at least ten years and a Georgia resident at least four years when they assume office. The attorney general also is required to have had seven years as an active-status member of the State Bar of Georgia, which supervises the legal profession in the state. The Constitution leaves it to the General Assembly to spell out the power and duties of these officers, to determine their salaries, and to fund their agencies.[26] It also sets forth a procedure under which four of the eight constitutional officers can petition the Georgia Supreme Court to hold a hearing to determine whether one of the other constitutional officers is permanently disabled and should be replaced.[27]

The six elected department heads possess power independent of the governor. They do so in part because of the prerogatives of their offices. The attorney general, for instance, exercises great discretion regarding the handling of litigation in which the state

is a party and issues opinions on the legality or constitutionality of actions taken by the state.[28] The insurance and agriculture
commissioners have substantial power to regulate certain types
of businesses. In addition to the power they derive from being
elected separately from the governor, the narrow focus of their
offices means that constitutional officers' natural constituencies
(for votes and campaign money) are the interests affected most directly by their decisions. In fact, they are often seen as advocates
for the industries they oversee.[29] Elected department heads may
even be in conflict with one another. Thus, despite the image of
governors being quite powerful, executive power in Georgia is dis-
persed.

CONSTITUTIONAL BOARDS AND COMMISSIONS

States commonly assign decision making in certain policy areas
to multimember boards rather than to departments headed by a
single individual. Georgia is no exception. The Georgia Constitution spells out the authority of eight boards (see table 6). Others
have been created by law or executive order.

The eight boards and commissions required by the Constitution are among the most powerful agencies in Georgia, in part
because any changes in their basic authority and membership require a constitutional amendment rather than passage of a law by
the General Assembly. The power of these **constitutional boards
and commissions** is also reflected in the resources they control.
In fiscal year 2013, for instance, the University System Board of Regents received $1.8 billion in appropriations from the state, which
was less than 30 percent of its budget of $6.3 billion. Some money
is earmarked in the Constitution: Article 3 requires that state motor fuel taxes, which were almost $787 million in fiscal 2013, must
be spent for "an adequate system of public roads and bridges."
That provides substantial power to the Department of Transportation, which received another $1.2 billion in federal funding in
its budget of just over $2 billion.[30]

The Constitution insulates these boards from political pressure to some degree by providing relatively long terms that are
staggered. In the case of the State Board of Education and the
University System Board of Regents, the governor is specifically

TABLE 6

Constitutional boards and commissions in Georgia

Board or commission	Members	Membership selection
Education	14	One member per congressional district appointed by the governor to seven-year terms subject to Senate confirmation.
Natural Resources	19	One member per congressional district and five at large (at least one of whom is from a coastal county) appointed by the governor to seven-year terms subject to Senate confirmation.
Pardons and Paroles	5	Appointed by the governor to seven-year terms subject to Senate confirmation.
Personnel	5	Appointed by the governor to five-year terms subject to Senate confirmation.
Public Service	5	Elected statewide on a partisan ballot for six-year terms.
Regents	19	One member per congressional district and five at large appointed by the governor to seven-year terms subject to Senate confirmation.
Transportation	14	One member per congressional district elected by majority vote of General Assembly members whose districts overlap any of the congressional district.
Veterans Services	7	Appointed by the governor to seven-year terms subject to Senate confirmation.

SOURCE: *Constitution of the State of Georgia*, art. 4 (for six boards); art. 8, sect. 2 (State Board of Education); art. 8, sect. 4 (Board of Regents).

prohibited from being a board member. Members of most constitutional boards and commissions are selected geographically. Assigning one seat per congressional district assures that South Georgia will have seats on boards that otherwise might be dominated by people from the Atlanta area. It also means that the size of a board can change as Georgia gets additional seats in the U.S. House of Representatives.

The Public Service Commission was originally created by statute in 1879 to regulate railroads. Today it is composed of five members elected statewide for staggered, six-year terms and regulates telephone services, utilities such as gas and electricity, telecommunications, and transportation such as trucking and rail. The

State Transportation Board may seem like the essence of pork-barrel politics, with one member chosen from each congressional district by the state legislators whose districts overlap it (and benefit from highway construction). Members of the remaining six boards are appointed by the governor.

The Judicial Branch

There are essentially fifty-one legal systems in the United States, one at the national level and a distinct system in each of the fifty states. Like the federal government and other states, Georgia has an elaborate system of trial and appellate courts (see figure 1).

Trial courts apply laws to the facts in specific cases, reaching decisions in criminal or civil cases. **Appellate courts** review the actions of trial courts to determine questions of law (whether statutes or constitutional questions were interpreted or applied correctly). Decisions in appellate courts are made by groups of judges

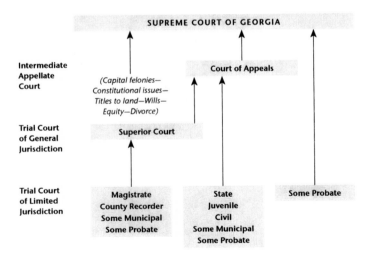

FIGURE 1. Structure of Georgia's court system. Adapted from the Judicial Council of Georgia and Administrative Office of the Courts, *1998 Annual Report on the Work of the Georgia Courts*, 12.

and do not involve witnesses or juries. The judges rely on written and oral arguments by the parties in the case being appealed, and some courts may permit other parties to submit written briefs in support of either side.

Unlike the U.S. Constitution, which grants Congress broad authority regarding the legal system, Article 6 of the Georgia Constitution includes specific detail about the operation of trial and appellate courts, the selection and conduct of judges, the election and performance of district attorneys, and a range of procedures. The Georgia Constitution requires that state judges be elected, primarily on nonpartisan ballots. Georgia's district attorneys, who are local officials responsible for criminal prosecutions, also are elected. This is quite different from the federal judicial system, where, subject to Senate confirmation, local prosecutors are presidential appointees under the authority of the U.S. Department of Justice and judges are nominated by the president, confirmed by the Senate, and can serve for life.

Georgia's executive and judicial branches are linked insofar as the governor is permitted to appoint people to vacant or newly created judgeships.[31] One study calculated that 66 percent of superior court judgeships between 1968 and mid-1994 were filled by appointment. Because judges are routinely reelected in Georgia and so many vacancies are filled by appointment, judicial selection in Georgia is often seen as a system of gubernatorial selection.[32] Another difference between the U.S. and state systems is that the Georgia attorney general can issue **advisory opinions**. These declarations advise agencies and local governments about whether actions they plan to take are legal; they have the force of law in Georgia unless overturned in court.

TRIAL COURTS

Georgia is often characterized as having one of the more complicated state court systems, in large part because of its many trial courts with limited jurisdiction. The Georgia Constitution grants the General Assembly discretion over the creation, jurisdiction, and operation of the state's courts, but it also requires that each county have at least one superior court, magistrate court, and probate court.[33]

A **superior court** is the trial court of general jurisdiction in each county that hears a broad range of serious cases, including divorces, felonies, and most civil disputes. The state is divided for administrative purposes into circuits that vary in population and size. Each county has its own superior court, but judges may handle cases in more than one county within a circuit. As workloads have increased, the General Assembly has added more judges and circuits.

Trial courts of limited jurisdiction hear specialized cases that are usually less serious than those in courts of general jurisdiction. These are primarily municipal courts dealing with traffic laws, local ordinances, and other misdemeanors. They also process warrants and may conduct preliminary hearings to determine if probable cause exists in a criminal case. Local acts passed by the General Assembly set courts' jurisdiction and the requirements for selecting municipal court judges.

The **probate court** in each county deals with wills, estates, marriage licenses, appointment of guardians, and involuntary hospitalizations of individuals. Probate courts may also issue warrants in some cases. Magistrate courts deal with bail, misdemeanors, small civil complaints, and search and arrest warrants. They also may conduct preliminary hearings.

Some counties have state and juvenile courts. The General Assembly passes local legislation to create state courts, which hear civil cases, traffic violations, or other misdemeanors. They may also hold preliminary hearings and act on applications to issue warrants. State courts operate in less than half of Georgia's counties and often have part-time judgeships. Small counties may not have a separate juvenile court judge and often call on superior court judges to serve in that role.

APPELLATE COURTS

Like most states, Georgia has two levels of appellate courts. Cases decided by trial courts may be appealed to the Court of Appeals, except in cases reserved for other courts; election contests, for instance, are exclusively under the jurisdiction of the Georgia Supreme Court.

The **Georgia Court of Appeals** was created in 1907 to relieve some of the burden on the Supreme Court. Its members are elected statewide on a nonpartisan basis for staggered, six-year terms. To help with an increasing work load, the General Assembly changed the state law, adding a tenth judge in 1996 and two more in 1999, resulting in today's court with twelve judges. The court often hears appeals on child custody, worker's compensation, and criminal cases that do not involve the death penalty. Cases appealed to the Court of Appeals are usually heard by a panel of three judges. If one of the judges on a panel dissents, however, a case may be heard by the full Court of Appeals.[34]

The **Georgia Supreme Court** comprises seven justices selected statewide in nonpartisan elections. They serve six-year terms. The justices choose whether to hear appeals from lower courts through the process of certiorari (request for information from lower courts). The Court has exclusive appellate jurisdiction over all cases regarding the Georgia Constitution, the U.S. Constitution as it applies within the state, elections, and the constitutionality of laws. It also may hear cases on appeal from the Court of Appeals and may be called upon to decide questions of law from other state or local courts. It has authority to hear appeals for all cases in which a sentence of death may be given. The Supreme Court is also involved in administering the state court system and regulating the legal profession.[35]

SELECTION OF JUDGES

The fifty states employ five methods for choosing judges: through partisan elections; through nonpartisan elections; by appointment of the governor; by election of the legislature; through a merit system in which nominating commissions screen candidates and submit them to the governor for selection.[36] Once in office, judges chosen under the merit system stand periodically for reelection.

Georgia has a long-standing commitment to electing judges, although there are requirements concerning age, place of residence, and membership in the State Bar of Georgia. The Constitution requires that members of the Supreme Court and the Court of Appeals be elected in statewide, nonpartisan elections for six-year terms. The justices of the Supreme Court choose a chief justice from among themselves. Superior court judges are also chosen in nonpartisan elections but serve four-year terms and are elected by voters who live within their circuits. State court judges are elected in nonpartisan, countywide elections for four years. Juvenile court judges are appointed, not elected, by the superior court judges of the counties they serve. The Georgia Constitution requires that all appellate and superior court judges be admitted to practice law for seven years prior to assuming their judicial positions. Voters approved an amendment to the Constitution in 2000, raising a similar requirement for state court judges from five years to seven.

The methods for choosing probate judges, magistrates, and municipal court judges are determined by the legislature through local legislation, which can vary widely. In Athens-Clarke County, for instance, the probate judge and magistrate are elected on a partisan ballot, but municipal court judges are appointed. Unlike the rest of the judiciary, the Georgia Constitution does not require probate judges, magistrates, or municipal court judges to have been admitted to practice law for a minimum number of years. It leaves such matters for the General Assembly to specify by law, which means that nonlawyers can serve in such positions. This has been a controversial issue, although state law does require certain training for those in such positions.[37]

The Constitution allows the Judicial Qualifications Commission to suspend, remove, or discipline judges who have been indicted or convicted of a crime, who cannot perform the duties of their office, or who have engaged in "conduct prejudicial to the administration of justice which brings the judicial office into disrepute." The Georgia Supreme Court must review the case before a judge can be removed from office.[38] Except in magistrate, probate, and juvenile courts, the Georgia Constitution authorizes the governor to appoint a replacement to serve the remainder of a judge's term when a position becomes vacant for any reason. The Judicial Nominating Commission assists the governor in making such appointments, and the selection process also includes input from political leaders and members of the legal profession.

District attorneys represent the state as prosecutors in all criminal cases and in all cases heard by the Supreme Court and

Courts of Appeals.[39] Qualifications for office include active membership in the State Bar of Georgia for three years. District attorneys are elected for a four-year term in each judicial circuit in Georgia. Thus, the average voter is expected to pick a prosecutor when the only information on the ballot is whether a candidate is a Democrat or Republican.

JURIES

The Georgia Constitution provides limited detail on juries, although it is significant that the matter is in Article 1 with the Bill of Rights rather than in the article on the judiciary, as it was in the Constitution of 1976. Citizens may be chosen to serve on grand juries or trial juries. While trial juries are the better known to the public because of television programs and media coverage of criminal cases, grand juries are important in determining how and if a case will proceed against a defendant.

Over half the states use a **grand jury** to issue an **indictment**, a formal charge accusing someone of a crime. Four states require grand juries for all indictments. Georgia is one of fifteen states that require a grand jury only for felony indictments. Six states require grand jury indictments only for capital crimes, and all other states make grand jury indictments optional, allowing the prosecutor to file an "information" in order to enter a formal charge.

Grand juries in Georgia consist of from sixteen to twenty-three members. In addition to issuing indictments, grand juries have broad powers to study the records and activities of county governments, issue reports, and make certain decisions. In deciding whether to issue an indictment, a grand jury must conclude that there is probable cause that the person committed the crime as charged. This is a far less rigorous standard than the "proof beyond a reasonable doubt" needed to convict the accused in a trial. Because the grand jury decides merely if sufficient evidence exists for an indictment, only the prosecution is heard, business is conducted in secret, and the defense has no right to cross-examine witnesses. Many have argued that this makes grand juries unnecessary and merely a "rubber stamp" for the prosecutor.

The Georgia Constitution calls for a **trial jury** of twelve members but allows the General Assembly to permit smaller juries and nonunanimous decisions in misdemeanor cases and in courts of limited jurisdiction. The size of the jury in Georgia is determined by the level of the court. Magistrate courts and juvenile courts never hold jury trials, and other lower courts are not likely to use juries. Superior courts have juries of twelve members. State courts have six-member juries. Juries in civil cases consist of six or twelve members, depending on the dollar amount of damages sought and, in state court, on whether either party requests a jury of twelve rather than six. Unanimous decisions are required in criminal cases, where the decision to use a jury rather than a judge for the verdict rests with the defendant. The General Assembly has other authority over the composition of juries. In 2005, for instance, legislators passed a law that gave the defendant and the prosecutor in a criminal case an equal number of "strikes" to remove potential jurors from a jury pool. Previously, the prosecutor was allowed only half as many strikes as the defendant.[40]

Local Government in Georgia

In addition to allocating authority among the three branches of state government, the Georgia Constitution also establishes a framework for the operation of local government.[41] This is especially important since the U.S. Constitution says nothing about the matter. Local governments in Georgia include a range of counties, cities, and special districts (see table 7).

COUNTIES AND CITIES

The Georgia Constitution is very detailed regarding local government, although it is somewhat more specific regarding counties than cities and special districts. Article 9 even restricts the number of counties to no more than 159, although no such limit applies to other local governments. The Georgia Constitution also requires all counties to have certain elected officials. These **local constitutional officers** include a clerk of the superior court, a judge of the probate court, a sheriff, and a tax commissioner (or a tax collector and a tax receiver), each of whom is elected to a four-year term. The Constitution leaves it to state law to spell out

TABLE 7

Number and type of local governments in Georgia, 1952–2007

Year	Counties	Municipalities	School districts	Special districts
1952	159	475	187	154
1957	159	508	198	255
1962	159	561	197	301
1967	159	512	194	338
1972	159	529	189	366
1977	159	529	188	387
1982	159	532	187	390
1987	159	531	186	410
1992	159	534	183	421
1997	159	534	180	473
2002	159	528	180	581
2007	159	530	180	570
2012	159	535	180	497

NOTE: Following consolidations such as those between Columbus and Muscogee County in 1971 and Athens and Clarke County in 1991, the U.S. Census Bureau counted the new governments as a municipality, not a county. They are also counted as counties here, however, because they retained their county functions and constitutional officers.

SOURCES: U.S. Census Bureau, *Census of Governments*, selected years. The census is conducted in years ended in 2 and 7. See http://www.census.gov/govs/go/.

the characteristics of local legislative bodies such as county commissions and city councils.

The Georgia Constitution goes to some length to prohibit counties from taking certain actions, such as those affecting local school systems or any court. It also lists services that cities and counties may provide, including public transportation, health services and facilities, libraries, and enforcement of building codes. This is especially important to counties, which were first authorized to provide urban services by a constitutional amendment ratified in 1972. Article 9 also allows counties and cities to adopt plans, enforce zoning, take private property, make agreements with one another, and consolidate.

SPECIAL DISTRICTS

Special districts provide a specific service or services over a defined geographical area independent of city and county governments. The Georgia Constitution permits a wide range of special districts, but their characteristics are covered by general laws. Probably the most visible special districts are local school systems. Policy making for education at the local level is the responsibility of elected school boards, who hire a superintendent as chief administrator. Prior to a constitutional amendment in November 1992, two-thirds of the county superintendents and 85 percent of the boards were elected.[42]

Perhaps the most important characteristic of special districts is their relative independence from county and municipal governments. For instance, areas can set up "community improvement districts" under state law to tax themselves for services beyond those that their city or county provides. There are districts for major malls in suburban Atlanta, and one district promotes physical improvements to the U.S. Highway 78 corridor in Gwinnett County.[43]

In addition to special districts that cover only part of a local government's geographic area, larger districts have been established to deal with regional issues. For example, MARTA (Metropolitan Atlanta Regional Transportation Authority) provides bus and subway service in Fulton and DeKalb Counties. The Georgia Regional Transportation Authority (GRTA) was created by the General Assembly in 1999 to oversee transportation and major development decisions in areas not meeting federal clean air standards.[44] As public needs and demands continue to arise, the General Assembly can use its constitutional power to create more special districts on top of the state's counties and cities.

HOME RULE

The Georgia Constitution provides **home rule** for cities and counties. In most states, this gives local governments broad powers to write and amend their charters (the equivalent of a local government's constitution) and to take any action not prohibited by the state. Home rule has proven more limited in Georgia, however. One study found that Georgia was one of twenty-five states in 1990 without a general law providing optional forms of government for counties, and one of twenty-six states that did not grant counties some autonomy in choosing their form of government. The same was true regarding municipalities, where Georgia was one of thirteen states that did not have a general law regarding optional forms of municipal government, and one of only ten that did not give cities any choice in their organizational structure. Unlike thirty states, Georgia did not divide its cities into "classes" (usually based on population), with different levels of authority granted to each class. Georgia does grant some flexibility to cities and counties in carrying out their functions.[45] In the end, local governments have some autonomy in day-to-day operations but little authority to determine their own organizational structure.

A major reason for local governments' limited power is the Constitution itself, which directly restricts counties and cities. It also permits the legislature to adopt local acts that apply to specific cities, counties, and special districts. Whereas some state constitutions prohibit them, local acts accounted for 48 percent of the bills passed in Georgia between 1980 and 2004. Local acts can cover a wide range of topics, even including the procedures for citizens to vote on merging governments in Athens-Clarke County and Augusta-Richmond County.[46]

LOCAL GOVERNMENT FINANCES

The Constitution generally leaves it to the General Assembly to determine how local governments can raise and spend money.[47] In contrast, the Constitution covers debt in substantial detail. Several of Georgia's restrictions on its local governments are common among the other states. First, debt cannot exceed 10 percent of the assessed value of taxable property within the jurisdiction. Second, the Constitution limits the annual amount that the jurisdiction can borrow on a short-term basis.

Third, a simple majority of voters must approve the issuance of new debt in an election. This applies only to **general obligation debt** (borrowing in which the local government pledges tax revenues to pay off bonds sold to raise money, usually for major construction projects). The voter approval requirement and debt limits do not apply to **revenue bonds**, which are not backed by taxes but by revenues from projects being financed by the bonds.

Airport revenue bonds, for example, are generally paid off with parking fees, aircraft landing charges, rents from airlines and concessionaires, and the like. With all types of local government borrowing, the real limit is the willingness of investors to buy bonds issued by a local government. In addition, local governments are required by state law to adopt a balanced budget each year.[48]

Georgia, like most states, limits local tax rates, mainly through laws passed by the General Assembly. State law allows counties and municipalities to levy a 1 percent general sales tax in addition to the 4 percent state tax. Local governments cannot levy the tax without the approval of their voters, however. Since 1985, counties have been permitted by law to use a 1 percent special purpose local option sales tax (SPLOST). The SPLOST is temporary, must be approved in a referendum, and must finance a specific list of projects such as streets and roads, bridges, and landfills.

In November 1996, Georgia voters ratified a constitutional amendment that allows school districts to collect a 1 percent sales tax for construction. This tax is similar to the SPLOST used by counties and must be approved by the school district's voters in a referendum. This new revenue source can generate millions of dollars of funds, especially in rapidly growing school systems, and help school boards reduce their debt and dependence on property taxes. Despite the narrow statewide majority ratifying the amendment, the tax quickly proved popular at the local level.[49]

CHAPTER 5

Elections

Just as constitutions specify the ways in which political institutions are organized, they also establish essential procedures such as elections. Article 2 of the Georgia Constitution provides basic ground rules for elections, such as the use of secret ballots and the establishment of eighteen as the minimum voting age (Georgia was the first state to adopt this minimum age, in the 1940s). Runoff elections and recalls are constitutionally established, as are procedures for removing and suspending public officials. However, the Constitution leaves most of the specifics regarding voter registration and election procedures to be decided by the General Assembly.

Types of Elections

PRIMARY AND GENERAL ELECTIONS

All states have **general elections** in which voters choose a person to fill an office. In most states, including Georgia, voters select each party's candidates for general elections in **primary elections,** which can often include many contenders. Some states also use party conventions to nominate candidates for certain offices. Primaries are not specified in the Georgia Constitution, but procedures are laid out by state law or political party rules.

RUNOFFS

In most states, the individual who receives the most votes in an election is declared the winner, but eight states, including Georgia require the winner of a primary or general election to receive a certain percentage of the votes cast.[1] Georgia's **runoff** was originally adopted in 1917 but has changed somewhat since then.

The logic behind the runoff system is based, in part, on the assumption that elections should reflect the will of the majority of the electorate. In places where there is a tradition of domination by one party with little or no opposition in the general election, candidates have faced their strongest opposition in primaries. If only a plurality were required, it would be possible to achieve elected office by finishing first in a primary with many candidates while still receiving well under 50 percent of the vote. To prevent that from occurring, the top two finishers face each other in a runoff, where the winning candidate gets a majority of the vote.

Traditionally, Georgia runoffs occurred after primaries, but in 1992 a runoff was held after a general election for the U.S. Senate. A third candidate prevented front-runner Wyche Fowler, the Democratic incumbent, from earning over 50 percent of the vote. His Republican opponent, Paul Coverdell, won the runoff. Since then, both political parties have changed the laws regarding runoffs in hopes of advantaging their candidates. The Democratic-controlled General Assembly adopted laws in 1994, 1996, 1997, and 1998 lowering the required vote in many elections to 45 percent. However, the requirement that a candidate get a majority or face a runoff was reinstated in 2005 after Republicans gained control of the legislature.[2] Runoff requirements also remain in many local elections.

Runoffs have been criticized as being biased against minority candidates, who might finish first in an election but not get a majority. A minority candidate could then be defeated in a runoff as whites voted in a bloc for the remaining white candidate. Runoffs have been the subject of litigation in Georgia. The U.S. Supreme Court permitted their continued use in 1999, however, when it refused to hear an appeal of a lower court ruling that the law requiring primary runoffs was not discriminatory.[3]

REFERENDUM ELECTIONS

States also conduct elections in which candidates are not running for office. The most common is a **referendum**, in which legislative bodies place issues on the ballot for the public to decide. Critics often complain that asking people to vote yes or no on a question is not a good way to decide complex issues. Georgia voters are accustomed to referenda on whether to amend the state constitution. At the local level, they are often asked to decide whether to adopt sales taxes, regulate liquor sales, or sell bonds to pay for public improvements such as roads and buildings.

REMOVAL OF ELECTED OFFICIALS

An election to remove public officials from office before their terms have expired is called a **recall election**. Georgia and seventeen other states allow recalling elected officials. Some states exempt certain officeholders, usually judges, from the recall process. In Georgia, all persons who occupy elected state or local offices, even if they were appointed to fill unfinished terms, are subject to removal. Recalls are placed on the ballot through a petition process established by law. If an office becomes vacant through recall, a special election is held to fill the position.[4]

The Constitution allows other means for removing public officials. The House of Representatives can impeach any executive or judicial officer of the state, as well as members of the General Assembly. If the House votes in favor of impeachment charges, a two-thirds vote in the Senate is required to convict and remove the official from office.[5] The Constitution also includes procedures for the temporary suspension of the governor, the lieutenant governor, any of the other six constitutional officers, or a member of the General Assembly indicted for a felony by a grand jury.[6]

TIMING OF ELECTIONS

The 1983 constitution set the dates for the first general elections after its implementation; it also gave the General Assembly power to change the dates.[7] The General Assembly has not exercised that power, so elections for state offices are held the first Tuesday after the first Monday in November of even-numbered years. The members of the General Assembly are elected for two-year terms, which means that elections for these offices are held at the same time as those for the U.S. House of Representatives. The governor and other statewide officeholders serve four-year terms and are elected in years when the presidency is not on the ballot, which can protect Georgia candidates if their political party has an unpopular presidential candidate.

The Constitution sets the length of terms for other elected officials but leaves it to the General Assembly to determine by law when judges and most local officials will be elected.[8] County elections in Georgia are generally held at the same time as major state and national races, but most city elections are held at different times, usually in odd-numbered years.

REDISTRICTING

Like other states, in a process called **redistricting**, Georgia redraws the district boundaries for its legislature and the U.S. House of Representatives every ten years, following the U.S. census. A similar process occurs for city councils and county commissions. **Gerrymandering** (the practice of drawing districts in order to achieve political outcomes) is one method by which incumbents may protect their political careers, minority political parties may be prevented from gaining legislative seats, rural or urban districts may dominate, or the voting strength of minority groups may be diluted.

Although it originated in Tennessee, the U.S. Supreme Court's 1962 decision in *Baker v. Carr*[9] affected Georgia profoundly. This ruling and subsequent decisions forced states to draw legislative districts on the basis of population rather than political boundaries such as county lines. The "one person, one vote" standard required districts of equal population, although slight variation is tolerated. The U.S. Supreme Court has also limited the use of race in drawing legislative districts. The courts have allowed mid-decade redistricting in Georgia.[10]

CHAPTER 6

Rights and Liberties

Constitutions do more than establish governmental institutions and basic processes such as elections; they also guarantee individual rights and regulate a government's ability to interfere with people's liberties. Rights and liberties are included in a constitution in order to protect such guarantees from being reduced or eliminated by simply passing a law. At a minimum, state constitutions may not infringe upon liberties and rights protected by the U.S. Constitution. Because of dual citizenship and the Fourteenth Amendment to the U.S. Constitution, states may grant their citizens broader rights.

Article 1 of the Georgia Constitution allows state courts to determine whether laws or actions comply with the Georgia or U.S. constitutions.[1] This process of judicial review is similar to that at the national level. Any law or administrative rule in Georgia, whether adopted by the state or by local governments, may be challenged in court. In addition, some private practices, such as the activities of businesses or individuals, may be challenged. Unlike the U.S. Constitution, which specifies most rights in amendments, a bill of rights has been an integral part of each of Georgia's constitutions since 1861. Article 1 in the 1983 constitution includes twenty-nine paragraphs covering "Rights of Persons."

The discussion below covers some of the major provisions in Georgia's bill of rights. Under each heading, the first section describes how Georgia courts have applied these guarantees. This is followed by a discussion of related federal court cases originating in Georgia. These cases often led to substantial changes not only in Georgia but throughout the nation.

The first section covers civil rights, which are often thought of as the freedom to participate in the political system. Civil rights are generally linked to the guarantee of **equal protection**, which is the basis for much of the litigation on representation and discrimination. The next three sections deal with civil liberties--the basic protection against unwarranted government intrusion into one's life. The final section deals with the right to privacy--a protection not written explicitly into either the U.S. or Georgia constitutions. Tables 8–12 summarize major federal court cases. Citations for decisions by Georgia courts are found in the endnotes.

Equal Protection

GEORGIA COURTS

The second paragraph in Georgia's bill of rights guarantees, "No person shall be denied the equal protection of the laws."[2] This language mirrors the Fourteenth Amendment to the U.S. Constitution. While the Georgia Supreme Court has held that the federal and state equal protection guarantees "coexist," the justices have acknowledged that the state may interpret the Georgia Constitution to offer broader rights than are available under the U.S. Constitution.

A great deal of the controversy over equal protection involves government classification of groups, with the courts being most vigilant regarding race and sex. In 1984, the Georgia Supreme Court found unconstitutional a law that provided benefits to children whose mothers were wrongfully killed but did not afford the same protection to children whose fathers were wrongfully killed. The Court also struck down Atlanta's program to set aside a share of contracts for minority- and female-owned businesses because the city failed to demonstrate the need for a race-conscious program.[3] Local governments have been able to adopt set-aside programs, however, after conducting studies that determine the effects of prior discrimination. Such policies remain highly contentious and must operate within guidelines laid out by the U.S. Supreme Court, which has become increasingly skeptical of such initiatives. Similar controversies have surrounded affirmative action in admissions decisions at Georgia's public colleges and universities.[4]

Perhaps more controversial have been several Atlanta ordinances dealing with gay rights. In 1995, the Georgia Supreme

Court held that Atlanta could create a registry of unmarried couples (both heterosexual and homosexual) and forbid discrimination based on sexual orientation. However, the Court concluded that the city exceeded its authority by extending insurance benefits to the domestic partners of city employees.[5]

FEDERAL COURTS AND DISCRIMINATION

On the surface, the Fourteenth Amendment would seem to prohibit discrimination based on race. Yet Georgia, like other southern states, used a number of strategies to disenfranchise black citizens from the 1870s to the 1960s. These included the poll tax, the white primary, and other restrictions eventually eliminated by federal legislation and court decisions.[6]

The **poll tax** required citizens to pay an annual levy to be eligible to vote, thereby making it harder for the poor to vote. Georgia had used a poll tax earlier in its history, but it became particularly restrictive when the 1877 constitution made it cumulative, which meant that anyone falling behind in the annual tax had to make back payments. The poll tax was not repealed until 1945, when Governor Ellis Arnall made it a major issue during the legislative session. In other southern states, the poll tax lasted until the Twenty-fourth Amendment to the U.S. Constitution banned it in 1964.

Perhaps the most blatant attempt to disenfranchise blacks was the **white primary,** which restricted voting in party primaries to whites when the Democratic party was the defender of segregation in the South from the 1870s to the 1960s. Blacks could participate in the general election. Their votes were inconsequential, however, because Republican opposition was seldom on the ballot. This made the Democratic primary the "real" election.

White primaries were adopted in some Georgia counties by the 1890s. Beginning in 1900, only whites could vote in the Democratic party's primary elections. In a 1927 Texas case, the U.S. Supreme Court held that it was unconstitutional for state law to restrict primary voting on the basis of race. Virtually the entire South was controlled by the Democratic party then, and party leaders thereafter used party rules to enforce the white primary. Unlike general elections, which are run by the government, primaries could be regarded as activities of political parties, which are "private" organizations.

Not until 1944 did the U.S. Supreme Court hold that party rules enforcing a white primary also abridged the right to vote based on race. A federal appeals court overturned Georgia's white primary the following year in *King v. Chapman*. Perhaps the most immediate effect of this decision was in Atlanta, where white business and political leaders began developing a coalition with the city's black middle class.[7]

Three other restrictions were included in the Disenfranchisement Act of 1908, which voters approved as an amendment to the Georgia Constitution by a two-to-one margin:

> The **literacy test** required that voters be able to read and explain any paragraph of the federal or state constitution; while the **property qualification** required ownership of 40 acres of land or property assessed at $500. The **grandfather clause** enfranchised men who had served in the United States or Confederate military forces and their descendants; no one could register under that provision after 1914.[8]

Implementation of the literacy test was in the hands of local election officials, who exercised great discretion, especially their power to purge voter registration rolls of those judged to be unqualified.

As the momentum to desegregate grew during the 1950s and 1960s, the Georgia General Assembly produced an array of legislation to forestall the process.[9] At one point, all state aid was removed from any public school that was integrated, and payments were authorized to parents of children who attended segregated private schools. In order to prevent blacks from attending college in the state, requirements for admission were set to include letters of recommendation from two former graduates of the institution to which a student was applying. Since no blacks had attended most of these institutions, such letters would be difficult to obtain. Although most actions by the Georgia General Assembly were struck down as unconstitutional, white parents were able to move to different school districts or to send their children to private academies that did not admit blacks.

TABLE 8

Major federal cases on discrimination

King v. Chapman 154 F.2d 450 (1946)	Building on a 1944 U.S. Supreme Court case covering Texas, the circuit court of appeals found that the rules of Georgia's Democratic Party, which restricted voting in primary elections to whites only, violated the equal protection guarantee of the Fourteenth Amendment.
Heart of Atlanta Motel v. United States 379 U.S. 241 (1964)	Upheld constitutionality of Title 2 of the Civil Rights Act of 1964, which prohibited racial discrimination in public accommodations.
Olmstead v. L.C. 527 U.S. 581 (1999)	The state's practice of involuntarily institutionalizing disabled individuals judged suitable to live in less restrictive settings violates the Americans with Disabilities Act of 1990.

Segregation was largely maintained until Congress passed the **Civil Rights Act of 1964**, but it continued in many respects long after that. The Civil Rights Act outlawed discrimination in public accommodations (hotels, restaurants, transportation, for example) by relying on Congress's enumerated power to regulate interstate commerce. In *Heart of Atlanta Motel v. United States*, the U.S. Supreme Court took a broad view of the U.S. Constitution's commerce clause and upheld the Civil Rights Act, which would be enforceable despite state segregation laws because of the supremacy clause in Article VI of the U.S. Constitution. The Court rejected the motel's claim that it was a local business. Because the motel served interstate travelers, its practice of refusing lodging to blacks was held to obstruct commerce, and the motel would therefore have to desegregate.

Not all discrimination falls under the Fourteenth Amendment. Congress has also passed laws dealing with characteristics such as religion, age, and disability. One of the leading cases regarding the disabled was based on the ways in which the Georgia Department of Human Resources had institutionalized people involuntarily after it was determined that such people could be placed in a community setting. In *Olmstead v. L.C.*, the U.S. Supreme Court held that such action violated the protection of the Americans with Disabilities Act of 1990.

FEDERAL COURTS AND EQUAL REPRESENTATION

Since the early 1960s, federal courts have been active in the process of drawing districts for legislative bodies. The courts have interpreted the equal protection guarantee of the Fourteenth Amendment to mean that one person's vote should have the same weight in an election as another person's; to do this requires districts of roughly equal population. In *Fortson v. Toombs*, the Court ruled that reapportionment for the General Assembly must be made on the basis of the population of the state rather than by county or other political boundaries. Each district must have roughly the same number of inhabitants. After four earlier challenges had failed, in *Gray v. Sanders*, the U.S. Supreme Court struck down the county-unit system as a violation of the Fourteenth Amendment's equal protection guarantee because the system malapportioned votes by underrepresenting urban residents. Other litigation also forced the General Assembly to redraw congressional districts in the state.[10]

Questions of representation have become increasingly linked to race since Congress passed the **Voting Rights Act** (VRA) in 1965. The VRA suspended use of literacy tests, allowed federal election examiners and observers, and required affected state and local governments to receive approval from the national government before making changes in their electoral systems. This "preclearance" by the U.S. Department of Justice is aimed especially at changes that might dilute the voting strength of minorities. In June 2013, however, the U.S. Supreme Court struck down major provisions of the Voting Rights Act and left it to Congress to decide if the law should be revised.[11]

The U.S. Department of Justice objected to congressional redistricting by the Georgia General Assembly following the 1990 census. After two unsuccessful attempts to redraw districts, state lawmakers finally satisfied federal guidelines to protect minority voting strength in the 1992 elections.[12] Ironically, in 1995 those districts were ruled unconstitutional in *Miller v. Johnson* because

TABLE 9

Major federal cases on representation

Gray v. Sanders 372 U.S. 368 (1963)	Held that Georgia's county-unit system violated the Fourteenth Amendment's equal protection guarantee because it malapportioned votes among the state's counties.
Fortson v. Toombs 379 U.S. 621 (1965)	Upheld a lower court's 1962 decision that the Fourteenth Amendment required seats in the General Assembly to be apportioned with districts of roughly equal population rather than being based on county or other political boundaries.
Miller v. Johnson 515 U.S. 900 (1995)	Invalidated Georgia's congressional redistricting following the 1990 census as a violation of the Fourteenth Amendment's equal protection clause because race was the predominant factor in drawing district boundaries. The General Assembly had created three black-majority districts, with the Eleventh District having a very irregular shape.
Georgia v. Ashcroft 539 U.S. 461 (2003)	Held that courts reviewing redistricting under the Voting Rights Act have to consider all relevant factors affecting minority voters, not just the chance of electing minority candidates.

race was a "predominant factor" in determining the district lines.[13] Similar litigation occurred following redistricting based on the 2000 census: in *Georgia v. Ashcroft*, the U.S. Supreme Court again required Georgia to consider factors other than race in drawing legislative districts.

Right to Life, Liberty, and Property

GEORGIA COURTS

Life, liberty, and property are the first rights listed in the Georgia Constitution. Similar to guarantees in the U.S. Constitution, they cannot be abridged "except by due process of law."[14] State courts have found this guarantee to be broader than under the U.S. Constitution.[15] Georgia courts traditionally have found that the state has the power to regulate businesses so long as the regulation is applied equally to all who engage in the same types of businesses and has some "rational relationship" to a valid purpose. Only when litigants are able to show that their due process has been violated can they convince the courts that government regulation is arbitrary or unreasonable. Thus, laws regulating the licensing and training of professionals have largely been upheld. The Georgia Supreme Court has held that a mandatory life sentence for a second drug conviction does not violate due process or equal protection despite statistical evidence that a larger percentage of blacks end up serving life sentences under the law.[16]

All states and the federal government have some power of **eminent domain** (the taking of private property for public use such as a highway), but they require that property owners be compensated. While most Georgia court decisions have permitted government to determine the size and use of land taken, restrictions have been imposed on compensation for property. The courts also have applied the notion of taking to regulation of private property, that is, government regulation may be so restrictive that it has the same effect as seizing someone's property. In this regard, the Georgia Supreme Court has reviewed a great many cases dealing with land-use regulation and has tended to favor property owners over cities and counties. There are no landmark federal cases from Georgia dealing directly with this issue, although the state has had major cases dealing with the related question of privacy, as is discussed later in this chapter.

Rights Related to Expression and Association

Georgia's bill of rights includes a number of provisions designed to allow people to hold and express opinions, to associate with others, and to participate in the political process. These include two paragraphs on religion, one on the press, another on the right to assemble and petition, and one on libel, which is not mentioned in the U.S. Constitution.

GEORGIA COURTS AND FREEDOM OF CONSCIENCE AND RELIGION

Religious freedom was the earliest liberty to be addressed by Georgia's constitution drafters. Even the Rules and Regulations of 1776 included a provision for freedom of religion. The Georgia Constitution includes somewhat different language from the First Amendment to the U.S. Constitution.[17] Perhaps the most striking difference is Georgia's limitation on religious practices: "but the right of freedom of religion shall not be so construed as to excuse acts of licentiousness or justify practices inconsistent with the peace and safety of the state."[18] Thus, courts in Georgia have at times limited freedom of religion, as when the Georgia Supreme Court found that freedom of religion did not include the distribution of literature in public. Nor has the Court extended freedom of religion to the use of controlled substances.

GEORGIA COURTS AND FREEDOM OF SPEECH AND THE PRESS[19]

Georgia courts have adopted a relatively broad interpretation of freedom of speech. For example, while the U.S. Supreme Court held that restricting the screening of movies was not in and of itself a violation of free speech, the Georgia Supreme Court found that an ordinance requiring approval of a censor before screening movies was unconstitutional in Georgia. The Court also held that it violated free speech to ban those between the ages of eighteen and twenty-one from premises with sexually explicit performances.[20]

Georgia courts have also had to interpret a 1996 state law regarding what is called a SLAPP (strategic lawsuit against public participation). This acronym describes private lawsuits against citizens speaking or writing about government-related business. Critics of SLAPPs often point to large or powerful firms suing citizens or neighborhood organizations in order to intimidate them from opposing the firm, such as in zoning and development controversies. The General Assembly passed the law with the stated goal of protecting freedom of speech and the right to petition government for redress of grievances. The law allows the defendants in such cases to have the lawsuit against them dismissed and to be paid for their expenses and attorney's fees.[21] The courts have held that this law does not protect someone publicizing a private dispute.[22] Rather, the protection applies to matters that are being considered by government or that might be an issue of public concern. This protection can extend from speaking out at a public hearing to statements made to the media.[23]

Free speech, as interpreted by the Georgia courts, has limitations. Indeed, the Georgia Constitution says that people "shall be responsible for the abuse of that liberty," as in cases involving incorrect publication of delinquent debt, inaccurate information regarding criminal activity, or the use of photographs for advertising without the subject's permission. The Georgia Supreme Court has upheld an injunction against antiabortion protesters on the ground that the protest was limited by reasonable restrictions regarding time, place, and manner. The Court has also held that picketing was not protected free speech when it included an illegal strike. The Court also upheld the state's "Anti-Mask Act," which targets groups such as the Ku Klux Klan by prohibiting intimidating or threatening mask-wearing behavior, despite a claim that the law violates a person's freedom of speech.[24]

The press does not have an unlimited constitutional right to withhold a confidential news source.[25] However, the media have been granted limited protection by a state law that allows reporters to be forced to turn over information from confidential sources only when the evidence is material and relevant, is necessary for one of the parties to prepare a case, and cannot reasonably be gathered by other means.[26] In terms of other publications, the Georgia Supreme Court has held that it violates free speech for a city to prohibit the distribution of printed materials to homes.[27]

Controversies have swirled around language or behavior that many people judge to be offensive. For instance, the Georgia Supreme Court struck down a state law attempting to outlaw bumper stickers considered profane as being too vague and a violation of free speech. Even greater debates have involved sexually oriented communication, particularly after the Georgia Supreme Court ruled that nude dancing was protected expression and overturned local regulations banning such entertainment as too broad or outside the authority granted to local governments.[28] To reverse this action, Georgia voters approved a constitutional amendment in 1994 to increase local governments' control over nude dancing through their power to regulate alcoholic beverages. A number of local governments subsequently adopted ordinances to prevent clubs with nude dancing from serving alcohol. The Georgia Supreme Court has held that such alcohol regulations do not violate the free speech rights associated with such entertainment.[29]

FEDERAL COURTS AND FREEDOM OF SPEECH AND THE PRESS

The U.S. Supreme Court has considered many cases dealing with the First Amendment's guarantees regarding religion, speech, the press, and association. Two major cases on obscenity originated in Georgia. In a 1969 decision, *Stanley v. Georgia*, the Court found that "the mere private possession of obscene matter cannot constitutionally be made a crime," which Georgia law had done. Police had a warrant to search Stanley's home for materials related to illegal gambling, and during the search they found allegedly obscene material. The state claimed that certain types of materials should not be possessed or read, and that obscene materials may lead to sexual violence or other "deviant sexual acts." The Court rejected these claims, holding that the state asserted the "right to control the moral content of a person's thoughts . . . but it is wholly inconsistent with the philosophy of the First Amendment."

In a 1973 case, *Paris Adult Theatre I v. Slaton*, the Supreme Court was asked to determine whether the state could ban a commercial theater from showing films considered obscene. In contrast to its decision on *Stanley*, the Court concluded that the state had an interest in "stemming the tide of commercialized obscenity." The Court held that it did not make a difference that the films in question were shown only to consenting adults and the business posted warnings of the films' content and prohibited minors from entering. Instead, the Court held that the state had a valid interest in "the quality of life and the total community environment, the tone of commerce in the great city centers, and, possibly, the public safety itself."

Cox Broadcasting Corp. v. Colin dealt with Georgia's law prohibiting publication of a rape victim's name. Pitted against each other were the desire to protect the victim's privacy and the freedom of the press. The Court held that it would violate press freedom to prohibit the publication of crime victims' names obtained from public records.

A major case about regulating public demonstrations also originated in Georgia. Forsyth County was the scene of several marches by civil rights supporters and countermarches by the Ku Klux Klan during the 1980s. To manage these events, the county commission adopted an ordinance requiring those seeking a demonstration permit to pay a fee for law enforcement protection. The county administrator had discretion to set the amount of the fee, which could not exceed $1,000. One group refused to pay a $100 fee and sued the county. In *Forsyth County, Georgia v. Nationalist Movement*, the U.S. Supreme Court found that the county ordinance contained no standards for the administra-

TABLE 10

Major federal cases on freedom of speech and the press

Stanley v. Georgia 394 U.S. 557 (1969)	Overturned state law making private possession of obscene material a crime. The Georgia law was held to violate the First and Fourteenth Amendments to the U.S. Constitution.
Paris Adult Theatre I v. Slaton 413 U.S. 49 (1973)	Held that banning the showing of allegedly obscene films to consenting adults in a commercial theater does not violate the First Amendment or the right to privacy.
Cox Broadcasting Corp v. Colin 420 U.S. 469 (1975)	Overturned the Georgia law prohibiting publication of the name of a rape victim obtained from public records.
Forsyth County v. Nationalist Movement 505 U.S. 123 (1992)	Invalidated a local ordinance requiring participants to pay law enforcement costs for demonstrations and empowering the county administrator to determine how much to charge a group seeking a permit for a demonstration. The court found fault with the ordinance because it granted excessively broad discretion to the administrator, who was required to examine the content of a group's message in determining the fee to be charged for law enforcement protection.

tor to follow and was thus unconstitutional because it "contains more than the possibility of censorship through uncontrolled discretion [and] the ordinance often requires that the fee be based on the content of the speech" of the group seeking the permit. Thus, regulation should not depend on the content of a group's message.

Rights of Those Accused and Convicted of Crimes

The Georgia Constitution includes several provisions to protect people in dealing with the state's legal system. These concern searches, seizures, and warrants by law enforcement officials; access to the courts, the use of juries, and a speedy trial; the rights to an attorney and to cross-examine witnesses in criminal cases; the right against self-incrimination; protection against excessive bail and "cruel and unusual" punishment; and a prohibition against double jeopardy.[30] Most of these guarantees parallel those in the U.S. Constitution's Bill of Rights, although Georgia has additional guarantees. For instance, the state bill of rights explicitly prohibits whipping and banishment from the state as punishment for crimes,[31] imprisonment for debt,[32] and being "abused in being arrested, while under arrest, or in prison."[33]

GEORGIA COURTS

One of the distinctions between the Georgia and U.S. constitutions is that the state offers additional protection to defendants against unreasonable searches and seizures by law enforcement authorities. In addition, Georgia has long recognized the right of indigents to have a lawyer appointed, although this right does not extend to civil cases.[34] A major problem with providing attorneys to poor criminal defendants has been in providing resources to make the guarantee work well.[35]

Like the U.S. Constitution's Fourth Amendment, Georgia's bill of rights provides a right against "unreasonable searches and seizures," adding that warrants may be issued only when there is "probable cause" and must specify where to search and what or whom to seize.[36] Over the years, however, state and federal courts have identified conditions when police can act without a warrant. In Georgia, court decisions have allowed the use of evidence seized without a warrant for roadblocks under specific conditions,[37] police investigations when a situation arouses an officer's "reasonable suspicion,"[38] when safety concerns or other circumstances might justify a pat-down by police,[39] when officers are responding to 9-1-1 or other calls,[40] when officers have just arrested a suspect or stopped someone for a seat belt violation,[41] and when evidence is in an officer's "plain view," "plain feel," or even smell, as with marijuana.[42]

Debates over warrantless searches have extended to the period of time after someone has been convicted of a crime. Specifically, the Georgia Supreme Court has held that requiring convicted felons to provide DNA samples does not violate their rights against **search and seizure** or their right to privacy.[43]

Arguments often are made that certain actions are **cruel and unusual punishment**. Georgia courts have held that punishment exceeding the crime is, in some cases, constitutional. For example, fines larger than amounts taken by theft have been permitted. In some instances, defendants have been banished from certain counties, but the Georgia Supreme Court has not upheld banishment from the state as a whole. Georgia's use of the death penalty was found to be unconstitutional in 1972 by the U.S. Supreme Court because the state did not have standards to protect against unequal application of capital punishment. Currently, Georgia law lists the conditions under which the death penalty may be sought and is in line with later U.S. Supreme Court rulings permitting executions. The Georgia Supreme Court, however, has considered it cruel and unusual punishment to execute someone who is mentally retarded,[44] but it has reached the opposite conclusion when considering life in prison for a second conviction for selling cocaine.[45]

FEDERAL COURTS AND SEARCH AND SEIZURE

Georgia has produced few major federal cases related to the search and seizure of people or evidence under the U.S. Constitution's Fourth Amendment. In 1997, however, the U.S. Supreme Court overturned a Georgia law requiring candidates for state office to pass a drug test, which the General Assembly had passed as part of its antidrug efforts during the 1980s. Walker Chandler filed to run as Libertarian party candidate for lieutenant governor in 1994 but refused to take the test. In *Chandler v. Miller*, the Court held that the drug tests did not fall within the category of constitutionally permissible suspicionless searches. Indeed, the Court found that the test was essentially "symbolic" rather than being directed at some identifiable problem that might demand such a search.

The other major case involving Georgia concerned a warrantless search. One of the situations for which the U.S. Supreme Court has held that police can conduct such a warrantless search without violating the Fourth Amendment is when someone grants permission for the search. In *Georgia v. Randolph*, however, police conducted a search over a man's refusal when his estranged wife granted permission to the police. The Supreme Court held that conducting such a warrantless search over an occupant's objections violated the Fourth Amendment protection against "unreasonable" search and seizure.[46]

FEDERAL COURTS AND THE RIGHTS OF CRIMINAL DEFENDANTS

The U.S. Constitution's Sixth Amendment includes the right to a fair trial, which is not spelled out in detail. Therefore, the courts have had to define what that right means in practice. Some of these cases have dealt with the size of trial juries and whether they must reach a unanimous decision. In a 1973 Florida case, the U.S. Supreme Court permitted six-member juries in civil cases. In *Ballew v. Georgia*, however, the Court ruled in 1978 that Georgia's use of five-person juries in misdemeanor cases violated the right to a fair trial, in part because of the reduced deliberation and bias in favor of the prosecution regarding hung juries. Georgia's current constitution allows the General Assembly to permit six-member juries in misdemeanor cases or in courts of limited jurisdiction.[47]

FEDERAL COURTS AND THE DEATH PENALTY

Two appeals to the U.S. Supreme Court from Georgia during the 1970s became the landmark cases regarding the use of capital punishment in the United States. The first, *Furman v. Georgia* in

1972, effectively ended executions throughout the country. Four years later, *Gregg v. Georgia* allowed the state's rewritten capital punishment law to stand, thereby opening the door for states to resume executions.

What was different about these two cases? The members of the U.S. Supreme Court had a range of views regarding capital punishment, but the major concern was how the death penalty was applied. In *Furman*, the Court was concerned with both the lack of guidelines for deciding when to impose a death sentence and the wide variation in its use for similar crimes. The states then began revising their laws, and the Court decided several cases in 1976

TABLE 11

Major federal cases affecting those accused or convicted of crimes

Chandler v. Miller 520 U.S. 305 (1997)	Held that Georgia's requirement that candidates for state office pass a drug test violated the Fourth Amendment protection against suspicionless searches.
Georgia v. Randolph 547 U.S. 103 (2006)	Police cannot search a home without a warrant when one occupant grants permission but another physically present occupant refuses to permit the search.
Ballew v. Georgia 435 U.S. 223 (1978)	Held that a criminal trial using a jury of less than six members violated the Sixth Amendment guarantee to a fair trial.
Furman v. Georgia 408 U.S. 238 (1972)	Held that Georgia's methods of administering the death penalty violated the Eighth Amendment's guarantee against cruel and unusual punishment. The decision effectively ended executions in the United States for more than a decade.
Gregg v. Georgia 428 U.S. 153 (1976)	Upheld Georgia's revised law on capital punishment, which limited the crimes for which the death penalty could be imposed and specified the factors to be considered and procedures to be used in deciding when to impose capital punishment.
Coker v. Georgia 433 U.S. 584 (1977)	Found that Georgia's imposition of the death penalty for the crime of rape was grossly disproportionate and thus a violation of the Eighth Amendment's ban on cruel and unusual punishment.
McCleskey v. Kemp 481 U.S. 279 (1987)	Rejected the claim that racial differences in the imposition of the death penalty violated the equal protection guarantee of the Fourteenth Amendment and amounted to cruel and unusual punishment in violation of the Eighth Amendment.

based on the new statutes. In *Gregg*, the Court upheld Georgia's new capital punishment law, in part because it required specific findings by the jury regarding the facts of the crime and the character of the defendant; it also stipulated a process for appellate courts to review death penalty cases.

Two other cases tested the constitutionality of the conditions under which Georgia imposed the death penalty. In *Coker v. Georgia*, the U.S. Supreme Court held that the death sentence for the crime of rape was grossly disproportionate to the offense and thus violated the Eighth Amendment ban on cruel and unusual punishment. In *McCleskey v. Kemp*, the Court confronted the issue of bias in imposing the death penalty. McCleskey presented a study showing that the use of the death sentence in Georgia was statistically related to the race of the murder victim and, to a lesser extent, the race of the defendant. This pattern, he argued, violated the Eighth and Fourteenth Amendments. The Supreme Court rejected these claims, citing appellate courts' review of cases with facts similar to McCleskey's case.

The Right to Privacy

GEORGIA COURTS

Like the U.S. Constitution, Georgia's does not mention a right to privacy. In 1904, though, Georgia became the first state to recognize a privacy right when the Georgia Supreme Court found this right in natural law and the guarantees of liberty found in the U.S. and Georgia Constitutions.[48] Privacy has been extended to the right of a prisoner to refuse to eat, even to the point of starvation, and a person's right to refuse medical treatment even if it was certain to lead to death.

FEDERAL COURTS

The U.S. Supreme Court first recognized a right to privacy in a 1965 Connecticut case dealing with government regulation of contraception. Since then, the courts have been forced to define the limits of privacy rights. These debates include two Georgia cases. *Doe v. Bolton* remains almost unnoticed today, but it was the challenge to Georgia's abortion law decided at the same time as

Roe v. Wade, the more widely known Texas case in which the Supreme Court held that the right to privacy included a woman's right to abortion.

The second Georgia case was *Bowers v. Hardwick.* In this case, Michael Hardwick challenged Georgia's sodomy law as a violation of the right to privacy as it applied to sex between consenting adults. He also argued that as a homosexual he faced a constant threat of arrest and prosecution. The Supreme Court rejected Hardwick's claim and upheld Georgia's sodomy law, which prohibited certain sexual acts but did not specify the gender or sexual orientation of the participants.

DUAL CITIZENSHIP AND THE RIGHT TO PRIVACY

Georgia's sodomy law provides a good example of the way in which dual citizenship can produce different rights under the U.S. and state constitutions. The Georgia Supreme Court reinforced the Hardwick decision in 1996, when it ruled, in *Christensen v. State,*[49] that the state's sodomy law did not violate Georgia's right to privacy. That all changed in 1998, however. Based on facts involving a heterosexual couple, in *Powell v. State* the Georgia Supreme Court held that "insofar as it criminalizes the performance of private, non-commercial acts of sexual intimacy between persons legally able to consent, [the sodomy law] 'manifestly infringes upon a constitutional provision' . . . which guarantees to the citizens of Georgia the right to privacy."[50] Shortly thereafter, the Court rejected the claim that Georgia's right to privacy also protected commercial sexual activity.[51]

Thus, while any given state's law criminalizing sodomy would not violate the federal right to privacy as applied in *Bowers v. Hard-*

TABLE 12	
Major federal cases on the right to privacy	
Doe v. Bolton 410 U.S. 179 (1973)	This is the less famous Georgia case decided along with Roe v. Wade. It overturned Georgia's ban on abortions as a violation of a woman's right to privacy.
Bowers v. Hardwick 478 U.S. 186 (1986)	Held that the right to privacy did not protect consensual homosexual sex from prosecution under Georgia's sodomy law.

wick, state courts around the country could consider such a law in violation of broader rights guaranteed in their state constitutions. That possibility changed rather dramatically in 2003, however, when the U.S. Supreme Court's *Lawrence v. Texas* decision overturned sodomy laws in those states that still had them.[52]

The most recent frontier in battles over privacy rights deals with medical treatment. For instance, a 1997 U.S. Supreme Court decision left the door open for states to either ban or allow doctor-assisted suicide. This produced a conflict when former U.S. attorney general John Ashcroft attempted to keep Oregon from implementing its law allowing the practice. In 2006, the Supreme Court held that federal laws regulating drugs did not authorize the attorney general to regulate physician-assisted suicide, which would fall under the authority of the states to regulate doctors and medicine.[53] In 2008, voters in the state of Washington approved a ballot measure to allow doctor-assisted suicide there. As suggested by the debates over assisted suicide, the 2005 disputes over the use of life support for Terry Schiavo in Florida,[54] and controversies over stem cell research, constitutional and political battles over medicine and privacy will continue.

The Continuing Significance of Georgia's Constitution

A constitution is not some kind of sacred or unchanging blueprint for government. Constitutions are essentially political documents. That is why individuals, businesses, political parties, and interest groups often fight vigorously about interpreting and amending them. For instance, by approving an amendment to create a state-sponsored lottery in 1992, voters gave the governor, legislature, and bureaucracy millions of dollars to distribute to programs and individuals. They also paved the way for firms to profit from the production, sale, and marketing of lottery tickets. Another amendment granted a property tax break for growing timber,[1] although voters rejected a similar proposal for blueberries in 1994 but ratified a tax break for larger timber holdings in 2008. The 1992 amendment requiring that local school board members be elected and superintendents be hired allows boards to recruit superintendents from anywhere. Under the old system of electing school superintendents in some counties, only local residents could run for the office.[2] The 2004 amendment to ban same-sex marriage meant that Georgia courts could not permit the practice based on other portions of the state constitution.

As the preceding examples demonstrate, constitutions distribute political and economic power. They also set policies that under other circumstances might be enacted simply by passing a law. Voters undoubtedly will face proposed amendments every even-numbered year as various interests try to modify the Constitution to achieve their ends. If voters ratify a large number of changes, the Constitution might become so littered with amendments that it is unwieldy and difficult to interpret. A second possibility is that Georgians will become so annoyed with proposals on the ballot that they rebel by voting no on amendments. Finally, interest groups and members of the General Assembly might regularly use constitutional change as just another way to achieve their political ends. If so, Georgians might treat amendment battles as an ordinary part of the election process even though it would not be on the scale of some western states' use of the initiative. None of these scenarios bodes well for the durability of the 1983 Georgia constitution.

NOTES

Preface

1. U.S. Census Bureau, "State and Local Government Finances, Summary: 2011" (July 2013), http://www2.census.gov/govs/local/summary_report.pdf; "Government Employment and Payroll" (annual), http://www.census.gov/govs/apes/; U.S. Office of Management and Budget, *Historical Tables, Budget of the United States Government, Fiscal Year 2014*, p. 25, http://www.whitehouse.gov/sites/default/files/omb/budget/fy2014/assets/hist.pdf#page=1&zoom=auto,0,366.

Chapter 2. State Constitutions

1. See John Dinan, "State Constitutional Developments in 2012," 3–11, in Council of State Governments, *The Book of the States 2013* (Lexington, Ky.: Council of State Governments, 2013).

Chapter 3. Constitutional Development in Georgia

This chapter draws heavily from Melvin B. Hill Jr., *The Georgia State Constitution: A Reference Guide* (Westport, Conn.: Greenwood Press, 1994). Rather than weighing it down with extensive endnotes, specific references are used only when necessary. Readers are urged to consult Hill's exhaustive work for more detail.

1. Constitution of the State of Georgia, art. 3, sect. 9, para. 6b.

2. Constitution of the State of Georgia, art. 3, sect. 9, para. 6c–j.

3. Constitution of the State of Georgia, art. 1, sect. 2, para. 8c.

4. Constitution of the State of Georgia, art. 7, sect. 2, para. 3e.

5. Constitution of the State of Georgia, art. 7, sect. 1, para. 3c.

6. Constitution of the State of Georgia, art. 7, sect. 2, para. 5.

7. Constitution of the State of Georgia, art. 7, sect. 1, para. 3d. Also see Hill, *The Georgia State Constitution*, 152–55.

8. Hill, *The Georgia State Constitution*, 49.

9. Constitution of the State of Georgia, art. 4; art. 8, sects. 2 and 4.

10. Constitution of the State of Georgia, art. 4, sect. 3, para. 2.

11. Constitution of the State of Georgia, art. 3, sect. 6, para. 7; *Goldrush II v. City of Marietta*, 267 Ga. 683, 482 S.E.2d 347 (1997).

12. Hill, *The Georgia State Constitution*, 56–59.

13. Hill, *The Georgia State Constitution*, 194–95; Constitution of the State of Georgia, art. 9, sect. 2, para. 4.

14. *Woodham v. City of Atlanta*, 283 Ga. 95, 657 S.E.2d 528 (2008).

15. Hill, *The Georgia State Constitution*, 99.

16. Constitution of the State of Georgia, art. 1, sect. 2, para. 5.

17. 5 U.S. 137.

18. Congress passed a law in 1996 giving the president limited line-item veto authority. The U.S. Supreme Court ruled that this action was unconstitutional, however, after President Clinton applied it to eleven laws. See *Clinton v. City of New York*, 524 U.S. 417 (1998).

19. On the changing location of the state capital, see Kenneth Coleman, ed., *A History of Georgia*, 2nd ed. (Athens: University of Georgia Press, 1991), 91, 96, 107, 208–9.

20. V. O. Key Jr., *Southern Politics* (New York: Vintage, 1949), 119–22; Hill, *The Georgia State Constitution*, 224–25.

21. For a thorough account, see Harold P. Henderson, *The Politics of Change in Georgia: A Political Biography of Ellis Arnall* (Athens: University of Georgia Press, 1991), 77–96.

22. For an example of the politics surrounding the use of local amendments, see the account of the 1970 consolidation of Columbus and Muscogee County in Arnold Fleischmann and Jennifer Custer, "Goodbye, Columbus," in *Case Studies of City-County Consolidation: Reshaping the Local Government Landscape*, ed. Suzanne M. Leland and Kurt Thurmaier (New York: M. E. Sharpe, 2004), 46–59.

23. Bill Montgomery, "New Constitution in Hands of Voters," *Atlanta Constitution*, November 2, 1982; Hill, *The Georgia State Constitution*, 15–23.

24. "A Constitutional Mess, " *Atlanta Constitution*, August 28, 1981.

25. Bill Shipp, "Do the State a Favor: Forget the New Constitution," *Atlanta Constitution*, August 15, 1981. On the shifting power of governors and the General Assembly, see Harold P. Henderson and Gary L. Roberts, eds., *Georgia Governors in an Age of Change* (Athens: University of Georgia Press, 1988), 199–207, 234–37, 267–69.

26. "Streamlined State Constitution," *Atlanta Constitution*, June 30, 1983; "New State Constitution Deserves Ratification," *Atlanta Constitution*, October 24, 1982.

27. *Woodham v. City of Atlanta*, 283 Ga. 95, 657 S.E.2d 528 (2008).

28. See the campaign disclosure reports filed with the Georgia Government Transparency and Finance Commission, http://media. ethics.ga.gov/search/Campaign/CCDR_Report_Summary.aspx?Name ID=7299&FilerID=NC2010000057&CDRID=32222&Name=Yes2SaveLi

ves,%20Inc.&Year=2010&Report=December%2031st%20-%20%20-%20
Ballot.

Chapter 4. Georgia's Governmental Institutions

1. Hill, *The Georgia State Constitution*, 70.

2. *Constitution of the State of Georgia*, art. 3. For comparisons to other states, see *The Book of the States*, chap. 3.

3. *The Book of the States*, 59–60.

4. Imposing term limits on state legislators became politically popular in the 1980s and 1990s. Nineteen states eventually adopted them, but state supreme courts ruled them unconstitutional in Oregon and Wyoming. State legislatures later repealed them in Idaho (2002) and Utah (2003). See National Conference of State Legislatures, "The Term Limited States," http://www.ncsl.org/legislatures-elections/legisdata/chart-of-term-limits-states.aspx, and "Members Termed Out, 1996–2010," http://www.ncsl.org/default.aspx?tabid=14842.

5. See Edwin L. Jackson, Mary E. Stakes, and Paul T. Hardy, *Handbook for Georgia Legislators*, 12th ed. (Athens: Carl Vinson Institute of Government, University of Georgia, 2001), 1–9.

6. *Constitution of the State of Georgia*, art. 3, sect. 2, paras. 1 and 2.

7. *Larios v. Cox*, 314 F.Supp.2d 1357; Doug Norse, "Most Approve of New Legislative Maps," *Atlanta Journal-Constitution*, March 27, 2004.

8. *Constitution of the State of Georgia*, art. 5, sect. 2, para. 7.

9. *Constitution of the State of Georgia*, art. 3, sect. 3. Although the president pro tempore can become president of the Senate, the lieutenant governorship is left unfilled until the next general election should the position become vacant (see art. 5, sect. 1, para. 5). On legislative leadership in other states, see *The Book of the States*, 64–67.

10. Jim Galloway, "How a Freshly Elected Casey Cagle Was Stripped of Power," *Atlanta Journal-Constitution*, November 26, 2010, http://blogs.ajc.com/political-insider-jim-galloway/2010/11/06/how-a-freshly-elected-casey-cagle-was-stripped-of-power/.

11. *Constitution of the State of Georgia*, art. 3, sect. 5, para. 8.

12. *Constitution of the State of Georgia*, art. 3, sect. 5, para. 2.

13. *Constitution of the State of Georgia*, art. 3, sect. 4, para. 11.

14. *Constitution of the State of Georgia*, art. 3, sect. 9.

15. The line-item veto is not in the section of the *Constitution of the State of Georgia* dealing with appropriations but in the part of the legislative article (art. 3, sect. 5, para. 13) covering use of the veto in the enactment of laws.

16. *The Book of the States*, 169–76.

17. On elected trustees or regents in higher education, see *The Book of the States*, 282–83; "University of Colorado Board of Regents," https://www.cu.edu/regents/; University of Nebraska, "Board of Regents," http://www.nebraska.edu/board.html.

18. See Margaret Ferguson, "The Governors and the Executive Branch," in *Politics in the American States: A Comparative Analysis*, ed. Virginia Gray, Russell L. Hanson, and Thad Kousser, 10th ed. (Thousand Oaks, Calif.: CQ Press, 2013), 208–50.

19. See *Constitution of the State of Georgia*, art. 5, sect. 1; *The Book of the States*, 154–55. For a brief history of the Georgia governor's office, see Edwin L. Jackson and Mary E. Stakes, *Handbook of Georgia State Agencies*, 2nd ed. (Athens: Carl Vinson Institute of Government, University of Georgia, 1988), 38–39.

20. *Constitution of the State of Georgia*, art. 5, sect. 2, paras. 8 and 9; art. 6, sect. 7.

21. *Official Code of Georgia Annotated* (hereafter cited as OCGA), title 45, chap. 5.

22. *The Book of the States*, 159–60. Some states require larger majorities to override taxing, spending, or emergency measures.

23. *Constitution of the State of Georgia*, art. 3, sect. 5.

24. *Constitution of the State of Georgia*, art. 5, sect. 4, para. 1.

25. *Constitution of the State of Georgia*, art. 5, sect. 3.

26. *Constitution of the State of Georgia*, art. 5, sect. 3.

27. *Constitution of the State of Georgia*, art. 5, sect. 4.

28. OCGA, title 45, chap. 15; Jackson and Stakes, *Handbook of Georgia State Agencies*, 63–69.

29. Rhonda Cook, "Oink If You Know the Secret Menu for Legislature's Wild Hog Supper," *Atlanta Journal and Constitution*, January 10, 1993, and "Legislators Being Feted in Daytona," *Atlanta Journal and Constitution*, February 13, 1993.

30. Governor's Office of Planning and Budget, "The Governor's Budget Report: Fiscal Year 2014," 322 and 386, http://opb.georgia.gov/sites/opb.georgia.gov/files/related_files/document/Governors%20Budget%20Report%20FY%202014.pdf.

31. *Constitution of the State of Georgia*, art. 6, sect. 7.

32. Georgia Supreme Court Commission on Racial and Ethnic Bias in the Court System, *Let Justice Be Done: Equally, Fairly, and Impartially* (final report, August 1995), 56.

33. *Constitution of the State of Georgia*, art. 6, sects. 1–4. For detail on Georgia's courts, see the website for the Administrative Office of the Courts, http://www.georgiacourts.org/.

34. *Constitution of the State of Georgia*, art. 6, sects. 5 and 7; Court of Appeals of Georgia, "History of the Court of Appeals," http://www.gaappeals.us/history/index.php.

35. *Constitution of the State of Georgia*, art. 6, sects. 6 and 7.

36. On differences in states' methods of selecting judges, see Melinda Gann Hall, "State Courts: Politics and the Judicial Process," 251–78 in *Politics in the American States*. On judicial selection in Georgia, see *Constitution of the State of Georgia*, art. 6, sect. 7.

37. Carrie Teegardin, "Policing of Judges Gets Less Funding," *Atlanta Journal-Constitution*, April 5, 2009.

38. On the Judicial Qualifications Commission, see http://www.gajqc.com/.

39. *Constitution of the State of Georgia*, art. 6, sect. 8.

40. Georgia General Assembly, "2005 Summary of General Statutes," http://www.legis.state.ga.us/legis/2005_06/05sumdocnet.htm, and the text of HB 170, http://www.legis.state.ga.us/legis/2005_06/pdf/hb170.pdf. Also see Jim Tharpe, "Parents' Grief Leads to a Victory," *Atlanta Journal-Constitution*, April 6, 2005.

41. *Constitution of the State of Georgia*, art. 9, sects. 1 and 2; Hill, *The Georgia State Constitution*, 184–200. For a general discussion, see Arnold Fleischmann and Carol Pierannunzi, *Politics in Georgia*, chap. 10, 2nd ed. (Athens: University of Georgia Press, 2007).

42. *Constitution of the State of Georgia*, art. 3, sect. 5, paras. 1 and 2; Douglas C. Bachtel and Laura Boatright, eds., *The Georgia County Guide* (Athens: Cooperative Extension Service, University of Georgia, 1992), 66–70; Laughlin McDonald, Michael B. Binford, and Ken Johnson, "Georgia," in *Quiet Revolution in the South: The Impact of the Voting Rights Act, 1965–1990*, ed. Chandler Davidson and Bernard Grofman (Princeton: Princeton University Press, 1994), 68.

43. Steve Visser, "A Taxing Decision," *Atlanta Constitution*, June 14, 1999; also see Georgia Department of Community Affairs, "Best Practices and Planning Success Stories," http://www.dca.ga.gov/development/PlanningQualityGrowth/programs/BestPractices.asp.

44. David Goldberg and Kathey Pruitt, "GRTA Occupies Hot Seat," *Atlanta Constitution*, June 4, 1999; Lucy Soto, "Public Still Skeptical about Transportation Board," *Atlanta Constitution*, June 7, 1999.

45. U.S. Advisory Commission on Intergovernmental Relations, *State Laws Governing Local Government Structure and Administration*, report M-186 (Washington: Government Printing Office, 1993), 7–9, 17–22.

46. See Fleischmann and Pierannunzi, *Politics in Georgia*, 184–87,

246–57; see Leland and Thurmaier, eds., *Case Studies of City-County Consolidation*, chaps. 3, 6, and 10.

47. Taxation, debt limits, and revenue bonds are covered in *Constitution of the State of Georgia*, art. 9, sects. 4–6. Also see OCGA, title 36, chap. 5 on the property tax, chap. 7 on the income tax, and chap. 8 on the sales tax.

48. OCGA, title 36, chap. 81, sect. 3b.

49. *Constitution of the State of Georgia*, art. 8, para. 4; also see James Salzer, "Georgia Voters Throw Weight Behind Desire for Better Schools with Sales Tax Approvals," *Athens Daily News and Banner-Herald*, October 19, 1997.

Chapter 5. Elections

1. Alabama, Florida, Georgia, Mississippi, Oklahoma, South Carolina, and Texas hold runoffs if no single candidate is able to capture 50 percent of the vote. North Carolina also employs runoffs but reduced the threshold from 50 percent to 40 percent in 1989. Virginia repealed its runoff requirement in 1969, and Louisiana abandoned runoffs in favor of nonpartisan primaries in 1975. Arkansas, Kentucky, Maryland, and Utah have also used the runoff in the past. Arizona adopted a runoff for statewide general elections in 1988. See Key, *Southern Politics*, 416–23; Charles S. Bullock III and Loch K. Johnson, *Runoff Elections in the United States* (Chapel Hill: University of North Carolina Press, 1992).

2. On the rules for runoffs in Georgia, see OCGA, title 21, chap. 2, sect. 501.

3. *Brooks et al. v. Miller et al.*, 158 F.3d 1230 (1998); *Brooks et. al. v. Barnes et al.*, no. 98-1521, cert. denied May 24, 1999; Kathey Pruitt, "Majority Vote Still Needed in Primaries," *Atlanta Constitution*, May 25, 1999.

4. OCGA, title 21, chap. 4. On recall requirements in all the states, see *The Book of the States*, 331–38.

5. *Constitution of the State of Georgia*, art. 3, sect. 7.

6. *Constitution of the State of Georgia*, art. 2, sect. 3.

7. *Constitution of the State of Georgia*, art. 3, sect. 2, para. 5; art. 5, sect. 1, paras. 2 and 3; art. 5, sect. 3, para. 1.

8. *Constitution of the State of Georgia*, art. 6, sect. 7, para. 1; art. 8, sect. 5, para. 2; art. 9, sect. 1, para. 3.

9. 296 U.S. 186 (1962).

10. In 2005, the legislature's major redrawing of Georgia Senate districts in Athens-Clarke County was designed to benefit Republicans. Lawsuits to overturn it were rejected in federal and state court. For background, see Blake Aued, "Districting Boundaries Will Remain,"

Athens Banner-Herald, November 7, 2006, http://onlineathens.com/
stories/110706/election_20061107050.shtml.

Chapter 6. Rights and Liberties

It does not seem necessary to include detailed citations to Georgia court
cases in a general work such as this. Therefore, each section will include
a citation to the appropriate location in Hill's definitive work on the
Georgia Constitution, plus updates from the *Official Code of Georgia
Annotated*. Many of these cases are discussed in more detail, with full
citations in the endnotes, in Fleischmann and Pierannunzi, *Politics in
Georgia*, 67–82.

1. *Constitution of the State of Georgia*, art. 1, sect. 2, para. 5.

2. *Constitution of the State of Georgia*, art. 1, sect. 1, para. 2; Hill, *The
Georgia State Constitution*, 33–36.

3. *American Subcontractors Association v. City of Atlanta*, 259 Ga. 14, 376
S.E.2d 662 (1989).

4. Doug Cumming, "Applicants Nervously Await Decisions," *Atlanta
Constitution*, March 25, 1998. Following years of litigation over policies
at the University of Georgia, the U.S. Supreme Court gave support to
the limited use of affirmative action in college admissions in two cases
involving the University of Michigan: *Gratz v. Bollinger*, 539 U.S. 244
(2003), and *Grutter v. Bollinger*, 539 U.S. 306 (2003).

5. Douglas A. Blackmon and Holly Morris, "Court Gives Split Ruling
on Gay Rights," *Atlanta Constitution*, March 15, 1995. This area of the law
could be in flux due to the 2013 U.S. Supreme Court decision in *United
States v. Windsor*, no. 12-307.

6. On the right to vote, see McDonald, Binford, and Johnson,
"Georgia."

7. For a thorough discussion, see Clarence N. Stone, *Regime Politics:
Governing Atlanta, 1946–1988* (Lawrence: University Press of Kansas, 1989).

8. William F. Holmes, "1890–1940," part 5 in *A History of Georgia*, 2nd
ed., ed. Kenneth Coleman (Athens: University of Georgia Press, 1991),
280.

9. For a good synopsis of postwar racial change, see Numan V. Bartley,
"1940 to the Present," part 6 in *A History of Georgia*, ed. Kenneth Coleman,
2nd ed. (Athens: University of Georgia Press, 1991).

10. *Wesberry v. Sanders*, 376 U.S. 1 (1964).

11. *Shelby County v. Holder*, no. 12–96 (2013).

12. See Hill, *The Georgia State Constitution*, 225.

13. Linda Greenhouse, "Justices, in 5–4 Vote, Reject Districts Drawn
with Race the 'Predominant Factor,'" *New York Times*, June 30, 1995.

14. *Constitution of the State of Georgia*, art. 1, sect. 1, para. 1; Hill, *The Georgia State Constitution*, 30–33.

15. *Suber v. Bulloch County Board of Education*, 722 F.Supp. 736 (S.D. Ga., 1989).

16. *Stephens v. State*, 265 Ga. 356, 456 S.E.2d 560, cert. denied 516 U.S. 849 (1995).

17. *Constitution of the State of Georgia*, art. 1, sect. 1, paras. 3 and 4; Hill, *The Georgia State Constitution*, 36–38.

18. *Constitution of the State of Georgia*, art. 1, sect. 1, para. 4.

19. *Constitution of the State of Georgia*, art. 1, sect. 1, para. 5; Hill, *The Georgia State Constitution*, 38–40.

20. *State v. Café Erotica*, 269 Ga. 486, 500 S.E.2d 547 (1998).

21. OCGA, title 9, chap. 11, art. 3, sect. 11.1.

22. *Georgia Community Support & Solutions v. Berryhill*, 275 Ga. App. 189, 620 S.E.2d 178 (2005).

23. *Providence Construction Co. v. Bauer*, 229 Ga. App. 679, 494 S.E.2d 527 (1997); *Harkins v. Atlanta Humane Society*, 264 Ga. App. 356, 590 S.E.2d 737 (2003); *Atlanta Humane Society v. Harkins*, 278 Ga. 451, 603 S.E.2d 289 (2004).

24. *State v. Miller*, 260 Ga. 669, 398 S.E.2d 547 (1990).

25. *Vaughn v. State*, 259 Ga. 325, 381 S.E.2d 30 (1989).

26. See OCGA, title 24, chap. 9, sect. 30.

27. *Statesboro Publishing Co. v. City of Sylvania*, 271 Ga. 92, 516 S.E.2d 926 (1999).

28. *Harris v. Entertainment Systems*, 259 Ga. 701, 386 S.E.2d 140 (1989).

29. *Goldrush II v. City of Marietta*, 267 Ga. 683, 482 S.E.2d 347 (1997).

30. *Constitution of the State of Georgia*, art. 1, sect. 1, paras. 11–24; Hill, *The Georgia State Constitution*, 42–51.

31. *Constitution of the State of Georgia*, art. 1, sect. 1, para. 21.

32. *Constitution of the State of Georgia*, art. 1, sect. 1, para. 23.

33. *Constitution of the State of Georgia*, art. 1, sect. 1, para. 17.

34. *Bergman v. McCullough*, 218 Ga. App. 353, 461 S.E.2d 544 (1995), cert. denied 517 U.S. 1141 (1996).

35. Jonathan Rapping, "National Crisis, National Neglect: Realizing Justice Through Transformative Change," *Journal of Law and Social Change* 13 (2009–10): 331–59; Stephen B. Bright and Lauren Sudeall, "Overcoming Defiance of the Constitution: The Need for a Federal Role in Protecting the Right to Counsel in Georgia," Issue Brief, American Constitution Society for Law and Policy, September 2010, http://www.acslaw.org/files/Bright%20and%20Lucas%20-%20Right%20to%20Counsel.pdf.

36. *Constitution of the State of Georgia*, art. 1, sect. 1, para. 13.

37. *Coursey v. State*, 295 Ga. App. 476, 672 S.E.2d 456 (2009).

38. *Lane v. State*, 287 Ga. App. 503, 651 S.E.2d 798 (2007); *State v. Jones*, 287 Ga. App. 259, 651 S.E.2d 186 (2007).

39. *Walker v. State*, 289 Ga. App. 657, 658 S.E.2d 207 (2008); *Carter v. State*, 287 Ga. App. 597, 651 S.E.2d 759 (2007); *Teal v. State*, 291 Ga. App. 488, 662 S.E.2d 268 (2008); *Johnson v. State*, 285 Ga. 571, 679 S.E.2d 340 (2009).

40. *Lester v. State*, 287 Ga. App. 363, 651 S.E.2d 766 (2007); *Edmond v. State*, 297 Ga. App. 238, 676 S.E.2d 877 (2009).

41. *Spence v. State*, 295 Ga. App. 583, 672 S.E.2d 538 (2009); *Schramm v. State*, 286 Ga. App. 156, 648 S.E.2d 392 (2007).

42. *State v. Venzen*, 286 Ga. App. 597, 649 S.E.2d 851 (2007); *State v. Cosby*, 302 Ga. App. 204, 690 S.E.2d 519 (2010); *Somesso v. State*, 288 Ga. App. 291, 653 S.E.2d 855 (2007).

43. *Quarterman v. State*, 282 Ga. 383, 651 S.E.2d 32 (2007).

44. *Fleming v. Zant*, 259 Ga. 687, 386 S.E.2d 339 (1989).

45. *Crutchfield v. State*, 218 Ga. App. 360, 461 S.E.2d 555 (1995).

46. *Georgia v. Randolph*, 547 U.S. 103 (2006).

47. *Constitution of the State of Georgia*, art. 1, sect. 1, para. 1b.

48. *Pavesich v. New England Life Insurance Co.*, 122 Ga. 190, 50 S.E. 68 (1904).

49. *Christensen v. State*, 266 Ga. 474, 464 S.E.2d 188 (1996).

50. *Powell v. State*, 270 Ga. 327, 510 S.E.2d 18 (1998).

51. *Morrison v. State*, 272 Ga. 129, 526 S.E.2d 336 (2000).

52. *Lawrence v. Texas*, 539 U.S. 558 (2003).

53. *Gonzales v. Oregon*, 546 U.S. 243 (2006). For more on the U.S. Supreme Court's view of assisted suicide and the right to privacy, see *Washington v. Glucksberg*, 521 U.S. 702 (1997), and *Vacco v. Quill*, 521 U.S. 793 (1997).

54. 544 U.S. 957. The case pitted the incapacitated woman's parent against her husband.

Conclusion. The Continuing Significance of Georgia's Constitution

1. *Constitution of the State of Georgia*, art. 7, sect. 1, para. 3e.

2. *Constitution of the State of Georgia*, art. 8, sect. 5, paras. 2 and 3.

ABOUT THE AUTHORS

Richard N. Engstrom earned his PhD from Rice University and has held faculty positions at Georgia State University and Kennesaw State University. He teaches and does research on state politics, elections, and public opinion. He is coauthor of the book *Quality of Life in the Atlanta Metro Area* (Burruss Institute of Public Service).

Robert M. Howard is a professor of political science at Georgia State University in Atlanta. He holds a law degree from Suffolk University and a PhD from the State University of New York at Stony Brook. His research interests include the influence of courts on tax and other public policy, courts and public opinion, and judicial decision making. He is the author or coauthor of three books and has published articles in law reviews and political science journals.

Arnold Fleischmann received his PhD from the University of Texas and was a member of the Political Science Department at the University of Georgia for twenty-six years. His research and teaching concentrate on state and local politics. With Carol Pierannunzi, he is coauthor of *Politics in Georgia*, second edition (University of Georgia Press). Since fall 2009, he has been head of the Department of Political Science at Eastern Michigan University.

Our thanks to **Carol Pierannunzi** for her help with the earlier versions of this monograph, as well as for her guidance with this effort.

CPSIA information can be obtained
at www.ICGtesting.com
Printed in the USA
LVOW10s1940141216
517267LV00002B/186/P